GRAMMA LARSC

Diary of
Love Poems

Enjoy Gramma's Love Poems

Aug Wolf

Helen O. Larson

Helen O. Wolf with her son Raymond in the 1940s

On the Cover: This is an image of Gramma Larson resting in front of her fire place. She is asleep and dreaming of her friend, lover, and husband Ivar. Their wedding picture seen on the mantle can also be seen on page 118. (Drawn by the author's sister, Ann Marie Wolf-Fox.)

GRAMMA LARSON REMEMBERS

Diary of Love Poems

Raymond A. Wolf

Featuring Poems by
Helen O. Larson

WOLF
PUBLISHING

Copyright © 2014 by Raymond A. Wolf
ISBN-13 978-1-4960-4862-2
ISBN-10 1-4960-4862-8

Published by Wolf Publishing
Hope, Rhode Island

Printed in the United States of America

For all general information:
E-mail: **theewolf@cox.net**

For orders:

Visit us on the Internet at: **www.raywolfbooks.com**

To my mom, Helen O. Larson
my inspiration and to
Ivar E. Larson
the greatest stepdad
any kid could every have

Contents

Acknowledgments

This book is written in remembrance of my mom, Helen O. Larson. Thank you for your beautiful poems. A great big thank you goes to my very talented sister, Ann Marie Wolf-Fox, for drawing the cover image of my mom resting in front of her fireplace, dreaming of her husband Ivar. This image depicts what *Diary of Love Poems* is all about. I wish to acknowledge the photographs Kimberly Roderick graciously loaned me. Also the support she offered me in my time of grieving. I wish to thank Jennifer Carnevale, for her tireless effort proof reading and being supportive and enthused of my latest endeavor. I wish to thank Ramona, my wife and partner, for understanding and being patient with my passion to publish yet another book of my mom's poems.

All photographs are from the author's collection unless otherwise noted.

Introduction

Gramma Larson often said, "People always tell me it is a gift the way I can write. I always respond saying I believe I am God's instrument to hold the pen to the paper as the words just flow out."

Helen O. Larson was known to friends and family as Gramma Larson. She was born Helen O. Francis October 24, 1910. She lived in a small New England Village named Rockland. It was located in the Town of Scituate, Rhode Island. The village existed for over 100 years until the City of Providence Water condemned it in 1916, by eminent domain, to build the Scituate Reservoir.

Helen wrote her first poem, *The Old School House*, at the age of twelve on the blackboard of her school as the workers were tearing it down. I feel compelled to include this poem as it started a lifetime of writing poetry that totaled 1,700. The last poem, *Couldn't Help Falling In Love*, she wrote two days before she passed away. It is also included as her closing poem.

When she finished the eighth grade she left school work behind to start working in the mill to help support the family. Her dad had already passed away at age 42.

Helen grew up and married Albert Wolf in 1936 to become Helen O. Wolf. They had two sons, Paul and Raymond.

They later divorced and to support her two sons, Helen traveled on the Pawtuxet Valley Bus line to her house cleaning jobs. One April morning in 1956 she started talking to the bus driver, Ivar E. Larson. She mentioned she really did not want to go to work that day. He replied don't go. She explained she had to, to support her two sons because her husband had left her. He commented his wife had left him and took his two daughters. This was the beginning of a love story but they did not know it. A few days later he asked if he could come up sometime and visit. She replied she had some brush that needed to be cut. If he would like to bring an ax and cut it, he would be welcome to come. Well, seeing he lived in an apartment he had to go out and buy himself an ax. She fed him supper that day and this scenario was repeated often.

On a cold snowy winter night in December 1957 the author stood up for them as they repeated, "till death do us part". They were happily married for 31 years.

Diary of Love Poems begins six days before Ivar passed away in 1988. She continued to live alone and write poetry until 2005. Gramma remarked a number of times, "I believe you can live to be too old". Her story concludes two days before she passed away seventeen years later.

I have chosen the most exceptional 103 of the 300 poems she wrote about her love for him during that time period. Some may make you cry, some may bring back memories of your own.

The photograph of Helen on the cover of *The Lost Village of Rockland*, in the Gramma Larson Remembers series, was taken in 1918 when she was eight. Four years later she would write the following poem. So, get comfortable in your favorite chair and enjoy *Diary of Love Poems*.

The Old School House

It was a very sad day when we were told
They were building a reservoir and our school would be sold

A man came one day, nailed up a sign for all to see
The sign read "condemned" it meant heartbreak for me

It was then we were told, an auctioneer would come one day
To auction off the old school house to be torn down and taken away

Then the day arrived, the auction took place
The people began to bid, tears rolled down my face

Going, going, gone the auctioneer cried
And on that fateful day something within me died

The old school house at Rockland, now is used no more
We hear no more footsteps walk across the floor

I'll come back now and then to reminisce and see
But the old school house at Rockland will be just a memory

Summer of 1923 – Age 12

One

The Beginning of the End

Diary of Love Poems begins six days before her husband, Ivar E. Larson, passed away. After being in the hospital for a long stay the doctors said there was nothing else they could do for him. She took her husband home against everyone's advice. They felt at 77 she was not capable of caring for him. However, she insisted and did so until his dying day. Her attitude was; "He took care of me when I was sick and I will take care of him now that he is sick." This photograph was taken in 1945.

This photograph of Ivar and Helen was taken March 1987. Less than one year later he became ill and spent eight weeks in Kent County Hospital in Warwick, Rhode Island. Helen took him home and cared for him until he passed away January 21, 1988. She then continued writing poetry about him, family, friends, Elvis, Jesus, and many events happening in the world. Her last and 1,700[th] poem, *Couldn't Help Falling in Love*, concludes this book.

The poems she wrote about her love for Ivar in this book are chronologically listed in order by date as she wrote them. They are numbered 1 to 300. Only the very best 115, in the author's opinion, are included in the following pages.

She wrote No. 1 six days before he passed away, January 21, 1988 and concluded with No. 300, on his anniversary, January 21, 2004, sixteen years later. The tone of her poems never changed and her love for him during this period never wavered.

Tears On My Pillow

My pillow is wet with tears
For I must say goodbye
To a pal so dear to me
And each night I cry

When night time comes again
My pillow will be wet once more
Because my dearest darling
You won't come in the door anymore

Why you had to get ill
The doctor said you must go
How I'll ever say goodbye
I really don't know

We were so happy dear
We laughed and joked each day
But it must be God's will
For I was told you cannot stay

We had so many good times
We bought some lovely things
Each time I look at them
Sad memories it brings

If my pillow should get wet
Once again tonight
I'll let it dry in the sunshine
Hoping I won't cry tomorrow night

So goodbye my darling
Soon you'll be in that land above
And when you go my darling
You'll take along my love

No. 1 - January 15, 1988 – Age 77
Six days later, Ivar passed away

Hospice

They're a volunteer group
They help where they can
They have banded together
To help their fellow man

My husband had cancer
They responded right away
In a few hours they were here
To help me through the day

So if you have a loved one
That has cancer some day
Please, call this number (401) 272-4900
They'll come right away

They'll bathe your loved one
Make the bed and do more
Thank God someone told me about them
I had never heard of them before

They have doctors and nurses
Medication and all services are free
Medication will be delivered to your home
As they did for me

And when your loved one passes away
They'll comfort you and stay
They'll hold your hand
And hug you for that day

So Hospice I humbly
Want to thank you
For responding so quickly
And staying with me until all details were through

No. 2 - January 1988 – Age 77

Two

The First Year Alone

This photograph of Helen was taken in the late 1940s in front of the house she helped build in 1942. All of the lumber including the shingles were cut at the Wolf family's saw mill. Helen did all the ordering of the doors and windows from the Champlin Lumber Company in West Warwick, Rhode Island. The cost for all of them was $500.00. The foundation was poured using a gasoline cement mixer and a wheel barrow. She lived the rest of her life in the house she loved.

Good Night My Love

You fell asleep my darling
Now we're so far apart
Though you are gone now
You're forever in my heart

You left so sudden darling
I didn't have time to say goodbye
I'm so glad you didn't suffer
But still I cry

I pray that you're in Heaven
And you can hear the Angels sing
I miss you so my darling
Each evening loneliness it brings

Someday I will see you
We'll hold hands once more
We'll hug and kiss each other
As we always did before

So good night my love
I must go to bed now dear
I'll try to go on living
Making believe you're here

No. 3 - February 4, 1988 – Age 77

Rocking Chair

I sit and rock alone
In my old rocking chair
Where you went I can't go
So I bow my head in prayer

You can't come back to me
So tears fill my eyes
For you went to be with Jesus
To His home in the skies

Darling I have memories
No one can take from me
In the evening I cry
So I can hardly see

Someday my dearest
I'll again be with you
When Jesus takes me home
When this life is through

You were so good to me
When I was sick you gave me loving care
So as the tears fall
I rock in my rocking chair

No. 5 - February 13, 1988 – Age 77

All Through Eternity

Some day God will wipe away
The tears from my face
And my loved one will be waiting
In that heavenly place

He will welcome me
With arms stretched out wide
I'll be forever reunited
For my love never died

He will be standing
With the angels in a robe of white
He'll beckon me to come to him
So he can hold me tight

So I'll live and wait
For that precious day
Where I'll hear my darling say
We're together this time to stay

Once again I'll be with my loved one
My darling you will see
We'll live and love forever
All through Eternity

No. 8 - April 1988 – Age 77

Goodbye My Darling

I brought my darling home
Each night I kneeled beside his bed to pray
Then early one morning
He closed his eyes and went away

Tonight my heart is breaking
I feel so all alone
Please forgive me Jesus
For wanting my darling home

I know it's wrong to want him back
I try to face the sorrow
But Jesus only you know
The hurt of tomorrow

We loved and laughed together
Each and every day
Jesus I shouldn't question
Why you took him away

To want him back again
It is wrong I know
Dear God please forgive me
I can't seem to let him go

I know there's a Heaven
Where there is no sin
Please ask the Angels to move over
And make room for him

No. 10 - 1988 – Age 77

Helen loved to paint things. Whether it was her furniture, doors, door frames or the outside of the entire house, which she did a number of times. The shingles having been cut at the saw mill were rough and did not like to hold paint. Eventually, she and Ivar had the whole house re-shingled. They then had an antique silver stain applied and never had to paint it again. The huge Oak and Elm trees that used to shade the house became diseased and had to be removed (see page 142). The terrace was built around them. This photograph shows the author (right) with his best friend Joseph D. Noel. It was taken in the 1950s.

Helen kept this carpenters apron from Champlin Lumber Company all these years. Champlin gave it to her in 1942 because she ordered all the doors and windows for the house from them, at a total cost of $500. The company has long been out of business. Interesting, we now have zip codes and the phone number beginning with VA (meaning Valley) would now be 821-6990.

Birthday Remembrance
Ivar E. Larson
1915 – 1988

Once again we'll walk in the moonlight
Once again we'll walk by the sea

Once again you'll hold my hand
As you walk along with me

Once again I'll hear your laughter
Once again I'll see you smile

Once again we'll be reunited
In just a little while

So until that day my darling
I'll try to go on without you

Once again we'll be together
When my life on Earth is through

No. 12 – July 1988 – age 77

The Empty Chair

Tonight I'm with my family
One chair is empty now
To get through the lonely days
I don't know how

One more plate is missing
A cup and saucer too
Help me precious Jesus
The lonely nights to get through

Today I'm one year older
I've turned seventy-eight
Tonight my dearest darling
You have passed through Heaven's gate

Jesus, please take care of him
He's with you up above
Fold your loving arms around him
He's the only man I ever loved

Soon I will join him
He'll hold his arms out wide
And the tears of happiness
I won't try to hide

I live in the same house now, so all alone
It's now only a house; it's no longer a home

I no longer hear your footsteps outside
To mend my broken heart, I have tried and tried

It seems I hear your car drive up to the door
It seems you're coming home, as you always did before

No. 14 – October 24, 1988 – Age 78

Sterling Silver Ring

I remember the day in June
And the gift you did bring
You opened a small velvet box
And I saw a little silver ring

I placed the ring on my finger
Overcome by emotion that day
I broke down and cried
Then brushed the tears away

It had red ruby stones
All around the ring
I felt like a princess
And that you were my king

I wore the little ring for years
It is more precious than gold to me
In a safe place I have put it away
And now from thieves it is free

I'll cherish the little silver ring
Because it came from you
When you gave it to me you said
It's a token of my love so true

Maybe it isn't very valuable
On the market a small price it may bring
But there isn't enough money in the world
That could buy my Sterling Silver Ring

No. 15 - November 1988 – Age 78

Forever In My Heart

Each day when the Sun goes down
And it's getting dark
My love I want you to know
You are forever in my heart

I miss your handsome face
I miss that charming smile
And as I go along each day
I imagine you're here for awhile

I miss your thoughtful ways
And the gifts you gave to me
Oh! My precious darling my eyes
Fill with tears so I can hardly see

I miss the sound of your footsteps
Coming to the door
I never knew I wouldn't
Hear them any more

Today and each day
You're forever in my heart
It doesn't seem my dear
That we're so far apart

I look about the rooms
That are in my home
And darling it doesn't seem
That I'm really alone

No. 16 - December 7, 1988 – Age 78

Three

The Next Four Years

This photograph of Helen was taken in 1947 in her front yard. The pile of logs was from the clearing of the land to build the house. The telephone pole to the right brought power to the house. They could not afford to pay Kent County Water Authority to bring water from Main Street to the house, a distance of 300 feet. Therefore, Paul their oldest son, used to take two buckets in his wagon to a neighbor, Everett Leach's house, and fill them with water from his well and return home. Water was finally connected in 1947 at the cost of $342.00.

Ivar Emmanual Larson was born on July 13, 1915 in Oak, Nebraska. After joining the Navy on April 1, 1942 and serving his country for three years, he settled in Rhode Island. He married, had two daughters, and later was divorced. He landed a job with the Pawtuxet Valley Bus Line as a driver. One day he started a conversation with a lady who rode his bus frequently. That lady was Helen O. Wolf. It was destined they were to be married. The round cake in this photograph is celebrating Ivar's 65th birthday in July 1980. The other cake reads: "Welcome Home Ray & Joel" and "FLA". This was congratulating the author and his 13 year old son on completing their 30 day, 1678 mile bicycle trip from Hope, Rhode Island to Ft. Meyers, Florida. They had just arrived home.

Ivar E. Larson
Birthday Remembrance
1915 – 1988

Some day in the future
We'll walk down lovers' lane once more
I see your loving face my dear
As they open Heavens door

I go out to the garage
Where you made many things
And darling I must tell you
So many memories it brings

My heart is slowly breaking
The tears won't stop my dear
I love and long for you
And wish that you were here

But God had other plans
It had to be I know
He needed you my darling
To weed His garden, so you had to go

Only those who have lost
Can know what I've gone through
Since you left our home
The day that I lost you

So good night my darling
If it's meant to be
I'll be with you again
And you will be with me

No. 23 - July 1989 – Age 78

Ivar E. Larson enlisted in the Navy on April 1, 1942 for 2 years. He served from May 30, 1942 through September 24, 1945. He served an extra year because of the war. At discharge he was stationed at the Quonset Naval Base in Davisville, Rhode Island. This is where he decided to take up permanent residence.

The Picture On My Dresser

The picture on my dresser
Stares at me each day
Why can't I pick it up
And throw it away

I want to take it from its frame
And tear it apart
Instead I pick it up
And hold it close to my heart

It's only made of paper
Why does it cause so much pain
When I know that he will never
Come back again

One day he gave me a picture
I held it close to my heart
I vowed that the picture and I
Would never part

The picture on my dresser
Is in a golden frame
Every time I look at it
I keep calling his name

When I retire and go to bed
It smiles at me each night
It's the last thing I see
As I turn out the light

No. 24 - 1989 – Age 78

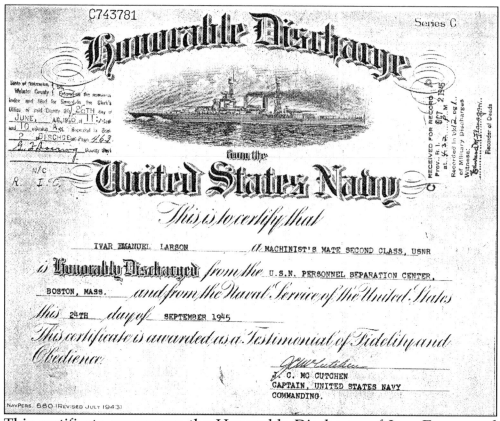

Honorable Discharge

from the

United States Navy

This is to certify that

IVAR EMANUEL LARSON, a MACHINIST'S MATE SECOND CLASS, USNR

is *Honorably Discharged from the* U.S.N. PERSONNEL SEPARATION CENTER, BOSTON, MASS. *and from the Naval Service of the United States this* 24TH *day of* SEPTEMBER 1945

This certificate is awarded as a Testimonial of Fidelity and Obedience.

J. C. MC CUTCHEN
CAPTAIN, UNITED STATES NAVY
COMMANDING.

NavPers. 660 (Revised July 1943)

This certificate announces the Honorable Discharge of Ivar Emmanual Larson on September 24, 1945 from the United States Navy. It also states it is awarded as a testament of Fidelity and Obedience.

The facing page shows the reverse side of this certificate. It affirms he enlisted on April 1, 1942 and entered active duty on May 30, 1942 thru September 24, 1945. It also records his monthly rate of pay at discharge was $100.80. Further, being discharged from Boston he was compensated travel allowance of .05 cents a mile to Edgar, Nebraska, his point of enlistment, for a total of $184.04. However, destiny decided he should stay in Rhode Island.

Enlisted as __S1c__   __4-1-42__
    (Rate)   (Date)

At __Denver, Colo.__   for __2__ years

Born __7-13-15__   at __Oak, Nebraska.__
     (Date)

Qualifications __those of rate__

4 Ratings held __S1c, F1c, MM3c, MM2c(T).__

Certificates __None__

Trade schools completed __None__

Special duties for which qualified __None__

Service (vessels and stations served on) or (served satisfactorily on active duty from

__5-30-42__ to __9-24-45__)

__NCTC, Norfolk, Va., NABD, Davisville, R.I., 5th Naval Const. Batt.,__

__CBRD, Camp Parks, Cal., R/S, Navy #128,__ Boston, Mass.

__Boston, Mass.__

<table>
<tr><td colspan="3">APPLICATION FOR
READJUSTMENT ALLOWANCE
PUBLIC LAW #346
MADE THROUGH
STATE __Rhode Island__
DATE __Oct 8 1945__
__618 36 99__
(Service Number)</td></tr>
</table>

Rating at discharge __MM2c(T)__ (CR 9-26-44) { Acting / Permanent }

Character of service __excellent.__   Final average __3.7__

H. E. Musgrave

H. E. MUSGRAVE , U. S. N. R.
COMMANDER.   and Executive Officer.

Height __5__ ft. __6__ in. Weight __152__ lbs. Eyes __Blue__

Hair __Light Brown__   Complexion __Ruddy__

Personal marks, etc., __S-3" left kneecap, anterior; S-1" left wrist; 2s½" cleft of chin;__
__VS-lt. forearm; S-2" left elbow, posterior;__

Is physically qualified for discharge. Requires neither treatment nor hospitalization.
I certify that this is the actual print of the right index finger of the man herein mentioned.

J. L. CHUTE, COMMANDER (MC) , U. S. N.
    and Medical Officer.

Monthly rate of pay when discharged __$100.80__

I hereby certify that the within named man has been furnished travel allowance at the rate of

__Five__ cents per mile from __Boston, Mass.__ to __Edgar, Neb.__

PAID $100 INITIAL M.O.P.

and paid $ __184.04__ in full to date of discharge.
(Amount)

Total net service for pay purposes _____ years _____ months _____ days.

<table>
<tr><td>RECORDED
WEST WARWICK
NOV 16 1951
WITNESS
Town Clerk</td></tr>
</table>

Ivar Emanuel Larson
(Signature of man.)

520004 N. I. Boyce , U. S. N.
    and Disbursing Officer.

29

In Memory Of My Husband
Ivar E. Larson
1915 - 1988

I brought you home my darling
It seemed you were getting well
But soon you would leave me
Though I had no way to tell

I'm thankful you didn't suffer
You just closed your eyes and went to sleep
And I was left a lonely widow
To face life alone and weep

I used to kneel beside your bed
And bow my head and pray
But God thought it was best
So he took you away

Now my only hope is that
We'll meet again some day
It's the only thing that keeps me going
Through each lonely day

Some day in the future we'll walk
Down lovers lane once more
I'll see your loving face
As they open Heaven's door

The wishing well you made for me
Stands in the yard alone
It's a silent reminder
That you're no longer in our home

I walk out to the garage where you made many things
And darling I want you to know so many memories it brings

My heart is slowly breaking; the tears won't stop my dear
I love and long to see you as it has passed another year

But God had other plans; it had to be I know
He needed you to weed His garden, so the flowers would grow

Only those who have lost can know what I'm going through
Since you left our home, the day that I lost you

How can I ever go on now you don't come in the door
Oh! If only you could come back and live with me once more

But since it can't be my darling I'll try to understand
And live one day at a time and do the best I can

You dedicated your body to medical science I know
There is no grave I can visit but you wished it to be so

No. 11 – January 21, 1990 – Age 79

Second Anniversary

Only One Man

God created a perfect man
And He gave that man to me
No other man can measure up
To the man that he used to be

He was my friend, my lover
All rolled into one
We loved, laughed and played
Until the setting of the Sun

Life is empty now
He's somewhere in the skies
My life with him on Earth
Was a paradise

Will I meet him some day
Will we hold hands again
Will I really recognize my love
When I see him

I look out the window
At the little path each day
Tears fill my eyes
As I stop to pray

Please dear God I ask you
To take the tears from my heart
There's so many tears there
Since we had to part

Goodbye my Dearest Darling
No one knows the pain
That I will have to bear
Until we meet again

No. 29 - April 15, 1990 - Age 79

It's Passed Another Year

My heart breaks a little more
With each passing day
The clouds of loneliness are closing in
Keeping the sun shine away

I walk out in the yard
Where we used to sit each day
One lawn chair is empty
For one day you were called away

The grass doesn't seem so green
The flowers seem faded and worn
The birds don't sing so sweetly
Since you've been gone

The clouds in the sky
Still roll by my dear
The seasons remind me darling
That it's passed another year

How can I ever go on
What can I ever do
To fill the empty space in my heart
That's been there since I lost you

You were so good to me
The best friend I ever knew
I keep wondering why
I had to part from you

Oh! To live once more that night we said I do
When we promised to always be faithful, loving and true

No. 30 – January 1991 – Age 80

January 21 - Third Anniversary

This photograph of Helen was taken in the fall of 1942. This was before the author's father poured the concrete for the terrace. It was built behind the boulders to the right of the picture. The completed project is seen on page 18.

She Walked That Path Again

She went for a walk in the woods
The sky over head was blue
The flowers were so pretty
Covered with morning dew

She saw a black crow
Sitting on a dead tree
And as she walked that path
It took her back in memory

She passed a babbling brook
The water was so clear
As she listened to the noise it made
It seemed you were so near

As she continued walking
She saw children at play
She could hear their laughter
As she walked along that day

She turned around and headed home
Leaving old memories behind
Of a love she'll remember
Until the end of time

As she entered her home
She said good night to him
If fate decides to let them
Some day they'll meet again

No. 31 - September 13, 1991 – Age 80

In Memoriam – Ivar E. Larson
1988 – 1992

It was in the month of April
The day I met you dear
Since the day you left me
It has passed another year

Oh! That beautiful day I met you
I'll remember for all time
And the angels must of smiled
The day you became mine

Thirty-one years passed so quickly
Then I lost you one day
Memories, Oh! Those memories
Are with me to stay

You were the greatest husband
Any woman could ever know
But God called you away
He willed it to be so

I brought you home one day
It seemed you were getting better
Six weeks I loved and cared for you
Then one day you slipped and fell

The last time you were with me you couldn't sit up that day
And only God and the angels know why you passed away

Now I am so lonely, no one seems to care
Do you look down and see me, from your home up there

No. 32 – January 21, 1992 – Age 81

Fourth Anniversary

The Sky Is Misty Blue

The sun is shining today
The sky is misty blue
As I sit in the sunlight
My thoughts turn to you

I remember the picture
You sent in the mail
Each day I think of you
My love will never fail

I think how much in love we were
I was yours and you were mine
And we kept our promise
To love for all time

The years have passed my darling
Your hair was silver gray
You have no way of knowing
How lonely I am today

You used to answer the phone
When I didn't hear it ring
I put you on a pedestal
You were my everything

You wasn't a king on a throne, no crown on your head
I remember that last evening and the heart breaking words you said

The sun is shining today, the sky is misty blue
As long as I live and breathe, I'll be in love with you

So I'll go on writing many poems about you
For you was my greatest love, all the years through

No. 34 - January 30, 1992 – Age 81

This photograph of Ivar was taken in June 1961 while he was reading the Sunday paper in his favorite chair. The kerosene stove to the right heated the parlor in the winter. The fireplace to the left was electric and only for show. The photograph on the shelf to the far right is of the author and the one on the far left is the author and his older brother Paul.

So Long Ago

Oh! Those walks in the moon light
Beneath the evening star
I long to see you once more
I wonder where you are

Come back to me my darling
And knock on my door
I hold on to old memories
As it was once before

I look at the chair where you sat
I glance at your picture again
Please call and say you are coming
Please knock and I'll let you in

Yes, I hold on to those memories
Of so long ago
For I love you much more
Then you'll ever know

I go to the mail box
Each and every day
Looking for a letter that will tell me
You're coming back some day

As I sit in the evening
By the candle light glow
I hold on to memories
Of so long ago

I live the nights again
When we used to dine
I thought to myself
I'm sure he is mine

I think of the evenings
Spent by the fire as the flames rose high
I never once dreamed
That you'd have to say goodbye

Oh! Those candle light dinners with just us two
Oh! Those precious moments I spent with you

Oh! Those nights of ecstasy, I won't let those memories go
Of a great love I had so long ago

No. 36 - March 4, 1992 – Age 81

By The Sea

Take me back to the beach once more
Let me linger once more by the sea
Let me kick off my shoes and walk
Where you used to walk with me

As the moon shines up above
And the stars sparkle in the sky
Let me dream of those happy days
Where we walked, you and I

As long as I live and walk on the earth
Those dreams will live with me
Of those romantic summer evenings
When we walked beside the sea

The wind blew in my face
Salt was in the air
I was in paradise, for you
Were walking with me there

Let me go back again
For a little while
And I'll imagine I can see
Your handsome smile

I will never be able to say
Goodbye to the sea
For those were happy times
That you spent there with me

So my greatest wish is
That just once more
You'll walk with me again
On that beautiful shore

No. 40 - March 14, 1992 – Age 81

40

Crying Over You

As I look at the sky
I'm sad as can be
And the clouds up above
Are crying with me

I stop now and then
To brush a tear from my eye
I can't forget the day
You said goodbye

I'm a prisoner of love
Since you went away
Darling I'm crying
Once again today

I walk down the lane
Where we walked before
Then once again darling
I cry some more

To forget you my dear
I try and I try
But memories come back
And I cry and I cry

So I'll go on sobbing and crying
It's the only relief I can get
For my lover I once knew
And can't seem to forget

The clouds are still crying
And I'm sad as can be
The clouds sent a few rain drops
To prove they're crying with me

No. 42 - 1992 – Age 81

Our Last Evening

One evening so long ago
Tears filled both of his eyes
I sensed he was trying to tell me
We'd never kiss again beneath the skies

I looked at him and these words
I said to him
My love this can't be goodbye
I know I will see you again

Christmas is coming so soon
I know you will be with me
Love had made me his slave
I knew I would never be free

But that was the night it happened
Sometimes true love just dies
He opened the gates of hell
And shattered my world of paradise

The heart breaking years have passed
I love him as I did from the start
And there's a place reserved for him
Forever in my heart

Tonight I looked at his picture and a tear rolled down my face
For the man that stole my heart, the day he gave me that first embrace

So I put his picture away as I gave it one last kiss
For the day I met that man and entered a world of bliss

Good night my darling, I know that dreams sometimes come true
So I'll keep on dreaming that someday, fate will send me you

No. 48 - 1992 – Age 81

42

Every Day My Darling

Every day my darling
I'm holding back the tears
It seems just yesterday you went away
But it's now over four years

You were so good and kind
To everyone you met
And that's the reason darling
I can't seem to forget

No one will ever know
No one can understand
To find someone like you
That you were a special man

My eyes are filled with moisture
I'm still holding back the tears
It seems I can never face
The lonely coming years

Many people tell me
Start your life again
Don't wait for someone else
You'll never find another like him

One day each year tears fill my eyes
When I recall the day we married and I entered paradise

You came into our home and filled an empty place
I hold back the tears when I see a picture of your face

I know one day my darling the tears will fill my eyes
For I can't forget the day you left me for your home in the skies

No. 50 - 1992 – Age 81

Moonlight Walks

As I walk along in the moonlight
The sky is crystal clear
It brings back nights of long ago
When you were here

They say that time will heal
And take away all pain
But it isn't true my dear
Since you can't walk with me again

Oh! If I could just one more night
Walk along with you
It would take away the heart-ache
Of loosing you

The moon is coming up tonight
I want to walk once more
I want to hold your hand
As I did before

If I live to be one hundred
Or one hundred and ten
I will never find another
Like my husband and friend

Oh! Will the time ever come
Will the pain ever go away
From loosing that special man
I met on a bus one day

I'll try to go on my darling
I'll walk in the moon light alone
I'll try to bear the pain
Until God calls me home

No. 55 - December 10, 1992 – Age 82

44

Four

Another Five Years

This photograph of Helen was taken in the front yard of her home on Richard Street in July 1942. This was just one month after she gave birth to her second son, Raymond on June 6th. Helen would have been 31 in the photograph.

Every Time It Snows

I looked out this morning
And snow covered the trees
I thought how beautiful they were
And that God had made all of these

I recall an evening long ago
When the snow was on the ground
It was a night in December
That my true love I found

Now every time it snows
And a snow flake hits my face
I recall a night so long ago
And the memory of your embrace

It's snowing again my darling
And as it falls from the skies
I recall old memories
And tears fill my eyes

It was in the month of January
That you were called away
My heart is slowly breaking
A little more each day

You were so good and kind
To everyone you met
They say time will heal
But so far I can't forget

Now every time it snows
And a snow flake comes down
I am so very lonely
And I wish you were around

No. 59 - March 25, 1993 – Age 82

Your Picture

Tonight I looked at your picture
I picked it up and held it close to my heart
And I wondered why one day
Destiny tore us apart

One day I put your picture
In a golden frame
Now my heart skips a beat
Each time I hear your name

All I have left of our love
Is this picture of you
It will be my consolation
All my life through

You seem to smile at me
From the stand where you sit
And though I try and try
I can't seem to forget

I'll forever treasure your picture
I look at it each day
And as tears fill my eyes
I wonder why you couldn't stay

Once again as I retire, I'll hold your picture close to me
And again I'll wonder why destiny did this to you and me

This picture of you darling is the most cherished possession that I own
And I'll forever be grateful that is sits on a stand in my home

Your handsome picture is so precious you see
And I'll be forever thankful that your picture lives with me

No. 65 - April 4, 1993 – Age 82

The Angels Are Crying Again

It's raining outside today
The Angels are crying again
For they know how much I miss you
And long to see you again

I know the rain water's the flowers
And fills the brooks each day
But I'm lonely when it rains
Since God called you away

It always fills my eyes
With wet salty tears
When memories take me back
To all those happy years

The rain just now is hitting
My window pane
The birds and squirrels know
I'm crying for you again

I'd trade all my tears
And everything I own
Just to have you back
Once more in our home

Please let the sun shine
The Angels are crying for me
Please help me to forget
The way it used to be

I try to go on darling
Each and every day
I try to fight the loss I have
Since God called you away

No. 67 - April 11, 1993 – Age 82

48

We Kissed and Said Goodbye

We kissed and said goodbye
Beneath the stars above
Please erase from my memory
All those nights of love

All those precious evenings
Beneath the blue sky
All those days of bliss
It was paradise

I can't seem to forget
Darling I try and try
Will heart-ache last forever
Because we said goodbye

We were not to blame for parting
Destiny controlled that night
I blame destiny because we parted
And because it didn't turn out right

Will we ever kiss again
Beneath the evening star
Or will it forever be
The way things are

Oh! That night of heart-break
When we said goodbye
Oh! If just one more night
We could kiss beneath the sky

I'll forever love you
You're in my memory to stay
The night we said goodbye
And you were taken away

No. 69 - April 19, 1993 – Age 82

Moisture On My Pillow

There was moisture on my pillow
When I awoke today
I must have cried myself to sleep
Because you went away

I glanced at the stand beside my bed
As your picture sits there
Then I folded my hands
And said a morning prayer

I pray to God and I tell Him
I'm lonely as can be
Since the day you went away
After saying goodbye to me

Oh! The heart-ache that I know
And I can't explain
Since I know my dearest darling
You can't come back again

You were the best friend
That I ever knew
Is it any wonder that
I fell in love with you

Jesus keep him in your care
From loneliness set me free
Fold your loving arms around him
Since he can't come back to me

It is time once more
To switch out the light
And I know they'll be moisture
On my pillow again tonight

No. 70 - April 26, 1993 – Age 82

I Walk Alone

As I walk alone in the moon light
I glance at the stars above
And as they twinkle and turn
I think of my one only love

It gets so lonely at times
I can't count the tears that I shed
Since happiness was taken from me
And left me loneliness instead

Where did all the years go
Since you first knocked on my door
It's difficult for me to accept
That I won't see you any more

You came into a broken home
And made our family complete
Oh! It was a happy day
When destiny let us meet

I try to go on my darling
But I'm living in the past
I try to remember the good times
And so sorry they couldn't last

I wonder where you are tonight, are you looking down on me
Can you see me sitting alone, lonely as can be

Oh! Darling I miss you so; I can't stand the empty space
Whenever I look at your chair, I long to see your face

If only you could come back again for just a short time
I'd tell you things I forgot to say dearest darling of mine

No. 71 - May 15, 1993 – Age 82

When You Come Back From Heaven

When you come back from Heaven
How happy I will be
To have you home again
Living with me

When you come back from Heaven
I'll welcome you home
I'll be happy once again
And I'll no longer be alone

Another robin came back
I heard him singing today
He's trying to tell me
You'll come back to stay

Is that the message he's bringing
Must I dare to hope once more
That someday very soon
You'll knock upon my door

I made many mistakes
Along the road of life
But it wasn't a mistake
The day I became your wife

When you come back from Heaven
And sit again in your chair
I'll be so happy darling
To know you're sitting there

I know I'm just dreaming
And that it can never be
But I can still make believe
You're coming home to me

No. 76 - 1993 – Age 82

Beside The Sea

I'm walking in the moon light
It's light reflecting on the sea
Once we walked beneath that moon
Just you and me

We once walked on that beach
Holding each other's hand
We were so happy then
As we walked on the sand

We used to listen to the waves
As they washed against the shore
Oh! To hold your hand
And walk with you once more

Then we'd watch the sea gulls
And listen to their screeching sound
Oh! What love and joy
On that beach we found

If only one more time I could
Capture that loving night
When we were so in love
And with our world all was right

Please come back my darling
And walk once more with me
Happy holding my hand
As we walk beside the sea

No. 77 - 1993 – Age 82

My Special Man

I look out the window each morning
I look out the window each night
I see the little path where you walked
But you're nowhere in sight

Must I go on each lonely day
Crying so I can't see
Must I face the coming years
And you're not with me

Jesus, help me to bear this burden
Please mend my broken heart
For darling it broke in two
The day we had to part

My darling there is no way
I could ever explain
The day you went away
And my heart filled with pain

I know that you would have never left
But God took you away
I also died a little inside
On that January day

Maybe someday I'll see you again
Once more I'll hold your hand
My heart is breaking so
For my special man

No. 78 - September 12, 1993 – Age 82

Jesus Catch My Tears

Every day I talk to Jesus
He's the only one who cares for me
He knows all my heart aches
And from tears will set me free

Each day as I look up
At the clouds in the sky
I pray to Him again
As once more I cry

Where are all the people
He told to watch His sheep
Why are they so silent
As a lonely widow weeps

Do they ever fold their hands
And for the lonely take time to pray
I wonder does anyone care
As I cry another day

Lord Jesus I don't mean
To sit here and complain
But I wonder how much longer
My body can take this pain

He was so kind and loving, your father made only a few like him
I was left a lonely widow to sob and cry again

Precious Jesus please forgive me for wanting my darling to come home
I look at each place where he sat, then realize I'm alone

Dear Jesus stay beside me, every hour of each day
And each time if I should cry, catch my tears as they fall away

No. 79 - October 10, 1993 – Age 82

55

Come Walk With Me

Come walk with me my darling
Along the beautiful shore
Come walk with me tonight
Come walk with me once more

Oh! Those walks we used to take
With your arm around me tight
Come walk with me again
Come walk with me tonight

I remember all those nights
That were so full of love
Walking along beside you
As stars shone up above

Come walk with me my darling
Your presence is near it seems
Come walk again with me
If only in my dreams

My heart is oh so sad
And so full of sorrow
Oh! My precious darling
Come walk with me tomorrow

The days and nights are lonely
The moon don't give her light
If only one more time
We could walk again some night

No. 83 - January 16, 1994 – Age 83

January 21 – Sixth Anniversary

It's Lonely Now

I sit alone my darling
It's so lonely now
I live one day at a time
I'll make it through some how

You were the best friend
That I ever knew
Is it any wonder darling
That I miss and long for you

When I was sick you cared for me
Like a mother cares for her child
You were so wonderful dear
You always had a smile

Now your chair is empty
Like the empty space in my heart
No one else can ever fill it
Why were we torn apart

The wishing well stands in the yard
You made it for me
Oh! Will I ever feel whole again
Will destiny be kind to me

The nights are so lonely
And each day is too
Darling the tears are about to start
So I must say good-bye to you

No. 86 - February 27, 1994 – Age 83

Jesus Knows

You see all the tears I shed
Now that I'm alone
You're in Heaven with your Father
Sitting on a throne

Jesus help me to go on
And face each lonely day
Tears roll down my face
Since your Father called him away

You know all the heart aches
That I have each day
You know all the tears
That I brush away

You look down from His home
High in Heaven above
You know how lonely I am
Since I lost my only love

He was so kind and loving
Your Father made only a few like him
I was left a lonely widow
To sob and cry again

Help me to go on each day
And when the tears start
I'll stop and pray to you
With a broken heart

No. 88 - March 26, 1994 – Age 83

When Roses Fade

Dearest darling I will love you
In the spring and every day
And when the roses bloom
I will love you after they fade away

And when the petals fall
And the wind blows them to and fro
I will still be in love with you
For I promised you so

The days are long and lonely
As I look at your empty chair
Oh! The hurt and the longing
To see you sitting there

Oh! To hear your foot steps
And to see you open the door
Darling I would be so happy
To see your face once more

The house is so quiet
I hear the clock tick away
Time passes so slowly
Since you were called away

Darling once again next year
Memories of you will return as the roses bloom
For in my heart you hold
A special little room

No. 91 - May 14, 1994 – Age 83

I'll Stop and Pray

When my heart is breaking
And I don't know what to do
Precious Jesus I can always
Stop and pray to you

Jesus you know all the heart aches
That I have each day
You know all the tears
That I brush away

You look down from your home
High in Heaven above
You know how lonely I am
Since I lost my only love

Precious Jesus I could never go on
If I couldn't talk to you
The days would be so long
And them I could never get through

Please forgive me if I have
Hurt someone today
Please forgive me for wanting
My Ivar to stay

Precious Jesus some how
I'll get through each day
And when the tears start again
I'll fold my hands and pray

No. 93 - 1994 – Age 83

God Called You Home

When the day starts
I walk alone
For one January day
God called you home

I see the birds
And the sunshine
But I lost that
Great love of mine

The sky is gray
It is never blue
Since that January day
That I lost you

My darling I try but
Life isn't the same now
But I manage to
Get through some how

So many places
We went together dear
Is it any wonder why
I want you near

Another day is starting
It's lonesome in my home
Another day of sorrow
Since God called you home

No. 96 - May 12, 1995 – Age 88

This photograph of Helen O. Wolf sitting beside the fireplace was taken in December 1945. This is the house she and the author's dad built in 1942 and she lived in until she passed away in 2005. The photograph of the curly haired boy in the sailor suit is the author. The next picture to the right is of the author and his older brother Paul. The last picture is again the author and his brother. This photograph was the inspiration for the drawing on the cover of this book.

Read Me A Story
(Bonus poem)

Read me a story mommy
A little boy said
Read me another story
Then I'll go to bed
Then I'll be good mommy
I will go to sleep
I will pray to Jesus
And ask Him my soul to keep
He grew up and married
And left the family home
And I sit here in my rocker
With my memories I'm alone

I do not see him often
He lives so far away
But memories keep coming back
And I can hear him say
Read me another story mommy
Please mommy dear
So I take out my hankie
And brush away a tear
Dear God watch over my boy
He's just three years old to me
And when the robins come back
Please send my boy home to me

About my son Paul in Watertown,
New York - Date Written Unknown

By The Fireplace

When the robins come back once more
And the grass once again turns green
I'll sit by the light of the fireplace
And once again I will dream

I'll dream of the way I wanted it
The way I thought it would be
That I wouldn't be sitting alone
But you'd be sitting here with me

Is it too much to ask
Is it too much to expect
Darling I dream and I long for you
For I can't seem to forget

The months and years have passed
Where can you be
Do you ever remember our love
Do you ever think of me

Another robin came back
I heard him singing one day
He's trying to tell me
You'll come back some day

Is that the message he's bringing
Must I dare to hope once more
That someday very soon
You'll knock on my door

So I'll go on hoping
It's the only way I can get through
Maybe fate will be kind
And one day I'll see you

No. 98 - 1995 – Age 84

Candle Light

I will set the table
I'll light the candles too
I'll use my best china
Then I'll wait for you

Will you come tonight
Will you dine with me
Will we hold hands across the table
Like it used to be

I know I'm only dreaming
We can never dine again
For he can't come to me
And I can't go to him

I gaze at his picture
He's so far away
He's still my dearest darling
I married one day

I'll blow the candles out
When the clock strikes nine
Then I'll retire and dream
Of that sweet heart of mine

I know he's safe where he is but I miss him so
How I long to see him no one will ever know

I opened the closet door to put my slippers away
It seemed I heard his voice and these words I heard him say

Don't cry my darling, I'll see you again
So I switched out the light and said good night to him

No. 99 - 1995 – Age 84

I Go Back In Memory

Let me go back in memory
To the day we first met
I try and I try dearest darling
But no way can I forget

Oh! That night that you told me
You wanted to marry me dear
It always brings tears to my eyes
Since you are no longer here

For destiny stepped in one day
And broke my heart in two
That's what happened my darling
The day that I lost you

I glance at your picture
Several times each day
As tears fill my eyes again
I turn and brush them away

Someday my true love
I hope to see once again
For God is the only one who knows
A part of me died with him

I looked at the chair where you sat; I had to put it away
I just couldn't take the heart-break, for you don't sit there today

I moved the other two chairs; they were used by my sons you see
To look at them every hour of the day brought tears to my eyes you see

Then I moved the kitchen table, where we ate and chatted each day
I miss you my darlings, I miss you, each minute, each hour of each day

No. 101 - 1995 – Age 84

If I Could Live Again

If I was to be born
In another life again
I would ask the angels to let me
Have one more life with him

He came into my heart
On a lovely spring day
And part of me died with him
When he passed away

I look at his picture
Every now and then
Wondering if I'll ever see
My true love once again

Just to see him once again
Walking in the door
Just to feel his loving arms
Around me once more

Just to feel the ecstasy
Of one more kiss
Just to live once more
In wedded bliss

But I know it can never happen
And he can't be with me
So I'll have to be content
With a beautiful memory

No. 102 - October 12, 1995 – Age 84

Some Day

Someday we'll walk again
Beneath the stars above
The moon will shine down on us
As once again we capture our love

I wonder where you are walking
Do you see the stars in the sky
Do you know when I walk alone
I stop to brush a tear from my eye

Someday we'll hold hands again
It will be as it used to be
Oh! What happiness we'll have
When you are united with me

I live for the day
I will see your face
And once again to know the thrill
Of your embrace

Someday the moon will be brighter
The stars will sparkle more too
When at last I am united
My darling with you

So until that beautiful day
Your memories will stay with me
And your picture will give me comfort
Until your face I see

No. 104 - January 18, 1996 – Age 85

January 21 – Eighth Anniversary

In Memoriam To My Ivar

I'd give all I own
If you could come home
And it was once more as it used to be
With you sitting in the lamp light with me

Oh! Darling if only
My wish could come true
And I could walk again
In the moonlight with you

I fell in love the day we met
It's a true love I can't forget
They say don't live in the past
But these memories will forever last

Oh! My darling, my heart
Is so filled with pain
For I'm longing to see
Your dear face again

I'm so lonely tonight
As I look at your chair
It's so empty now
For your not sitting there

As I gaze at your picture day after day
Tears fill my eyes and I brush them away

I try to go on and show a brave face
But it's only a mask, then tears take its place

Someday my love, we'll meet again
So I'll try to go on each day until then

No. 105 - February 7, 1996 – Age 85

I Can't Get You Out Of My Heart

I can't get you out of my heart
I try day after day
But the tears and heart-ache my darling
Just won't go away

I think of the love we shared
And the nice things you did for me
And darling I know, yes I know
From heart-ache I'll never be free

You were so kind to everyone
You changed my sad life to joy my dear
So is it any wonder my darling
That I wish you were here

I'll never forget you my darling
I try, yes I do try
But when evening comes again
I'll cry, I know I'll cry

I look at the chair where you sat
I look in the room where you used to sleep
My darling the pain won't go away
My darling the pain is too deep

Oh! Precious Lord Jesus, will peace ever come
To this broken heart of mine
Or will the pain and heart-ache go on
Until the end of time

Today the pain is with me
Today once more I'll cry
Lord help me to forget the day
I had to say goodbye

No. 107 - November 28, 1996 – Age 86

Memories

The autumn leaves are falling
They cover all the ground
My thoughts go back in time
To the great love I found

We loved and laughed together
And there were tears now and then
Oh! Where has that happiness gone
That I shared with him

Oh! If only for one hour
Or only one day
I could relive the love I had
That destiny has taken away

Often I glance at his picture
When I am alone
Often my heart aches for
The man who shared our home

Folks tell me to forget
And not live in the past
But these memories will be with me
As long as my life will last

Often tears are in my eyes
So I can hardly see
Goodbye my darling Ivar
You were so good to me

No. 108 - 1997 – Age 86

Five

The Year 1998

This photograph of Helen was taken in her front yard in June of 1961. She is all dressed up and ready to attend her son Raymond's graduation from high school. Helen always liked growing flowers, either marigolds or irises. Beside the flowers in the bird bath, she had flower pots lining the edge of the terrace. She also liked her cement animals, the duck on the terrace and the doe on the door step can be seen above.

Two friends that everyone knew, Ernest "Kit" Archambault and Adolph "Skee" Jusczyk, started the Pawtuxet Valley Bus Lines in 1953. Later in the 1950s they flew to Indiana, bought the bus in the photograph above and drove it home. They then proceeded to number it 50. The line ran from the village of Hope to the shopping center of Arctic to make connection with the United Transit Company (UTC) bus line going to Providence. It would then continue to Crompton in West Warwick and return back to Hope. The round trip took exactly one hour providing everyone on the route hourly service. This is the bus Ivar drove. It is pictured on Main Street in front of the Hope Post Office at the intersection of Route 116. The sign announcing the United States Post Office, Hope, R. I. can be seen above the bus on the building.

The header on the top of the front of the bus reads CROMPTON – HOPE. It was nearly at the end of the line where it would turn around by Hope Mill to start its run back to Crompton. Before starting back Ivar would roll up the header to read HOPE – CROMPTON. The advertisement on the front of the bus reads Warwick Club Beverages – Delicious Orange Soda. It contained a picture to the left, of an orange with a big smile, two eyes and a straw hat. The car parked to the rear of the bus is a 1959 Chevrolet.

This is the bus on which an acquaintance turned into a romance that grew into a love that lasted their lifetimes.

This photograph was taken by the author in 1960.

I Met Him On A Bus

I met him on a bus
It was early in the spring
I had no way of knowing
What the future would bring

I said I don't feel like going to work
He said then don't go
I told him I had two sons
So it has to be so

He said his wife left him
For a sailor she met
And memories of that first meeting
I will never forget

One day he asked
If he could come and see me
I told him I was married
But would soon be free

Well, he brought an ax
And came one night
And he cut down trees
As long as it was light

And very soon we fell in love one night
And we ate many dinners in the evening light

Then one day he said, will you marry me
I was so very happy that destiny had meant it to be

I have some letters and a picture and today I live alone
Since the day in January, God called my darling home

No. 109 - January 13, 1998 – Age 87

This photograph pictures left to right, Ivar, Helen, the author and his son Joel. It was taken on August 16, 1986 at the authors wedding at Shepherd of the Valley Church in Hope. Joel stood up for his father as the best man. Later in July 2000 the author was Joel's best man.

My Darling Ivar

If I was to be born
Into another life again
I'd ask God to let me
Have one more night with him

He came into my life
Early one spring day
And a part of me died with him
When he passed away

It was so hard for me
To say goodbye that day
I knew my heart would be broken
Each and every day

I look at his picture
Every now and then
Wondering if I'll ever see
My true love once again

I keep his loving picture
In a drawer in my hutch
Oh! My precious darling
I loved him so much

So I'll say goodnight
And put his picture away
And with a broken heart
Tomorrow I'll face another day

No. 110 - January 21, 1998 – Age 87

Ten years have passed, the eleventh begins

Ivar is shown here with another bus parked in the company garage in West Warwick. The photograph was taken by the author in July 1956. The company grew and added a second bus to the Hope to Crompton line providing service every half hour to their customers. Later "Kit" and "Skee" (see page 72) started a large charter division. As the business grew they started a school bus division and secured contracts with local towns. As there was no need for the small commuter line any longer, it was dropped in the 1960s. By the early 1970s Skee had sold his share of the business to Kit. Kit eventually brought his son Steven into the business. In September 1997 they merged with Coach USA. As of this writing, Steven still manages the bus company, now named Academy.

My Bus Driver Husband

I go back in memory
Each and every day
To the day I stepped on his bus
Early one spring day

I said, I don't feel like going to work
The bus driver said, don't go
I said, my husband left me
So it has to be so

I said, each and every day
I feel so all alone
But I have two good sons
So I'm trying to make them a home

He said, my wife left me
For a sailor that she met
He said, I understand
That it's so hard to forget

We talked each morning
He seemed such a nice man
He asked if he could come
With an ax to clear the land

One beautiful day he said will you marry me
So just before Christmas we married and celebrated around
a Christmas tree

Oh! That handsome bus driver that I met so long ago
I fell in love right away and destiny allowed it to be so

The driver I met on the bus, I married one night
And 31 years we had happiness, each and every night

No. 111 - November 1, 1998 – Age 88

Destiny Changed My Life

It was on a bus that I
Met this man one day
We talked each and every morning
Then I fell in love with him one day

He asked if he could come and see me
With an ax to clear the land
I didn't know that one day
He'd place a ring on my hand

He kept his promise to come
And so one day he came
And from that blessed day
My life was never the same

Both of us were so happy
As we ate in the candle light
And I will forever treasure
The memories of that night

He said to me
I must be going now
I'll be back again to see you
Tonight I make a vow

And he kept his word
And came the next night
And my love and I always
Ate in the evening light

No. 112 - November 15, 1998 – Age 88

My Night In Paradise

Oh! That beautiful December night
When I married that man
I was in paradise when
On my finger he placed a wedding band

He promised to always love
And care for me each day
And he kept his promise
Until he passed away

We used to collect dishes
A pretty shade of blue
That man was so kind
And his love was so true

All through the years
We lived in wedded bliss
And you can't always find
A true love like this

We used to hold hands
When we watched TV
Oh! My precious darling
Was so good to me

Almost eleven years have passed
Now I live alone
Today I have only memories
Of the man who shared my home

No. 114 - November 24, 1998 – Age 88

My Precious Ivar

He came into my life
At a time that I was blue
He said if you will marry me
I'll always be good to you

And so one beautiful night
So many years ago
I married my precious Ivar
God willed it to be so

We went to church together
And to yard sales too
Oh! My darling Ivar
I'm so lost without you

As the sun comes up
And again when it goes down
I try to forget
One day cancer they found

I brought you home my darling
You came home to die
More than ten years have passed
And I'm left alone to cry

He was my husband
He was my friend
And he kept his promise
Right to the end

No. 115 - November 27, 1998 – Age 88

When Stars Come Out At Night

When stars come out at night
And I'm all alone
My thoughts go drifting back
To the day God called you home

I watched you each day
So brave and so kind
You just went to sleep
For all time

Six weeks I loved
And cared for you
And when the end came
I felt that I died too

Oh! My precious darling
I'm so lonely now
I'll try to go on
I'll get through the day some how

You were so kind to everyone
You went out of your way
To do something good
For someone each day

When the stars come out tonight
My thoughts will turn to you
And I'll always thank God
I had a love so true

No. 116 - November 28, 1998 – Age 88

To Walk Again In The Moon Light

Oh! If only one more time
I could walk in the moon light again
Just once more to capture the love
I had with him

So many years have passed
I'm so lonely today
Just once more, "I love you"
I wish I could hear him say

Just to feel his arms
Around me one more time
Just to see him once again
That precious husband of mine

Maybe I will see him again
Maybe he is waiting for me
Maybe he is also
Waiting to see me

I'm so glad I brought
My darling home one day
I'm so glad I cared for him
Until he passed away

So I'll go on dreaming
That someday I will see
My precious darling
That gave a wedding ring to me

No. 117 - November 29, 1998 – Age 88

The Day I Said Goodbye

When the moon
Comes up in the sky
Memories take me back
To the day I said goodbye

I wanted so much
For you to stay
But God called you home
On that January day

I walked out of your room
I thought you went to sleep dear
The nurse walked in and said
He's no longer here

When I lost you my darling
I lost my best friend
The day when your life
Came to an end

Life is so lonely
Now without you
I had to say goodbye
To my love so true

My heart is heavy
Since I live alone
God thought it best
So He called you home

No. 119 - December 3, 1998 – Age 88

Destiny I'm Crying

Destiny I'm crying
Once again today
Why have you followed me
All along life's way

When I finish crying
One more thing
You show up and
Tears to my eyes you bring

Can't you understand
Or don't you care
When I think all is well
You show up there

Destiny please stay
Away from me forever
It would be wonderful
If I didn't see you again ever

Destiny I'm crying
Once again today
You show up in all I do
And all I say

Destiny I'm crying
I'm crying once again
For you won't let me forget
That one day I lost him

No. 122 – December 8, 1998 – Age 88

84

Destiny Took You From Me

I'd give all I own
If you could come home
And watch television with me
Then I wouldn't be alone

My darling I wonder where you are
Are you safe and happy above
If I could send a letter to you
I'd send you my love

Oh! The things we did together
We were so happy each day
I feel so lost and lonely
Since God called you away

I'm so glad I brought you home
You were where you wanted to be
Oh! My precious darling
You spent your last hours with me

If I could only call you back
If I could have your love once more
If I could just once again hear
Your footsteps near the door

But destiny can't let it happen
I know you can't come home
I'll pray and look at your picture
Then I won't feel so alone

So my precious darling
I'll try to face each day
But it is embedded in my memory
The day you were called away

No. 123 - December 9, 1998 – Age 88

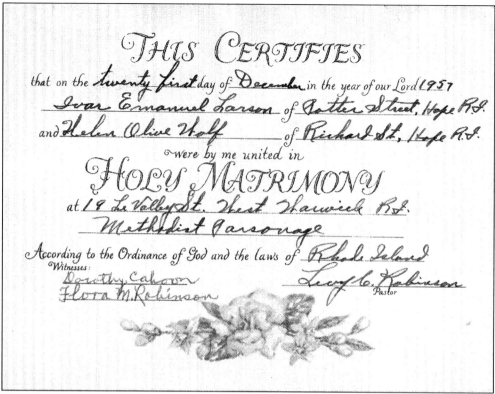

This is a copy of the original Holy Matrimony Certificate. It was signed by Pastor Leroy C. Robinson at the Methodist Parsonage at 19 LeValley Street in the Village of Phenix, Town of West Warwick. The witnesses were Helen's long time friend, Dorothy Cahoon and the Pastors wife Flora M. Robinson. The author recalls the cold and snowy Saturday, December 21, 1957.

Forty-One Years Ago

Oh! Let me go back to that night
Forty-one years ago when
We stood in a parsonage and
Promised to love to the end

You looked so handsome my dear
Dressed in a suit of blue
I thought I had died and gone to Heaven
When I heard you say I do

Then the pastor said
Repeat after me
And I made a sacred vow to stay
With you as long as my life would be

The Christmas tree was lighted
The guests were drinking wine
And on that cold December night
I married that sweetheart of mine

Those years of love and happiness
So fast they passed away
When at last I was left alone
With heart-break each day

That perfect night of happiness
When he was here with me
Will stay with me forever
For it's embedded in my memory

No. 125 - December 13, 1998 – Age 88

So then are they no more twain, but one flesh. What therefore God hath joined together let not man put asunder.
Matt. 19:6.

And Boaz took Ruth, and she was his wife. *Ruth 4:13.*

These verses were printed inside the Holy Matrimony certificate folder.

Her price is far above rubies. The heart of her husband trusteth in her. She doeth him good and not evil all the days of his life. *Prov. 31:10-12.*

Husbands love your wives, even as Christ also loved the church and gave himself up for it. *Eph. 5:25.*

Thirty-One Years Of Happiness

He promised he would spend
The rest of his life doing things for me each day
And he kept his promise
Until he passed away

He took me to malls
To buy things I liked too
What a wonderful husband
He'd do anything I wanted to do

He took me to yard sales
We got some good buys
He kept the promise he made to me
Until the day he died

I miss that man of mine
He had a heart of gold
And he was good to other people
I have been told

If I could only bring him back
To live with me once more
If I could only hear
His footsteps at my door

But he can't come back
And live with me
Destiny stepped in
And took him away you see

No. 126 - December 14, 1998 – Age 88

89

This photograph shows Ivar standing beside their green 1974 Plymouth Scamp. He and Helen used to travel around the Rhode Island country side looking for yard sales and antique shops. They loved to be able to add to their collections of Blue Willow dishware and Kerosene lamps. They maintained extensive collections of both. This photograph was taken in the early 1980s somewhere in their travels.

This photograph was taken in the late 1950s. From left to right are the author, Ivar, and the author's brother Paul. They are standing in front of Paul's 1956 Ford Fairlane Victoria.

90

The Green Car

I remember the very day
That we bought that car
It seems just like yesterday
He drove it near and far

We used to go to yard sales
And get some bargains too
And every time I think of it
I think of you

We used to go to church in it
Every Thursday night
It took us every where
In the dark and daylight

He had an accident once
And bent the door
But it still ran good
And in it we went once more

Oh! That beautiful green car
I miss it so today
But he isn't here to drive it
So it was towed away

I watched as they
Hooked a chain to tow it with
But the memory of that green car
Will stay with me as long as I live

No. 129 - December 16, 1998 – Age 88

The Sound Of Footsteps

If I could only hear the
Sound of your footsteps at the door
If I could have one wish granted
It would be to hear them once more

It's been so long my darling
Since you went away
It's still in my memory
The day I wanted you to stay

You used to take me for rides
And to buy pretty things
And in a little drawer
I keep our wedding rings

It takes me back in memory
When you were here with me
To have you here my darling
It wasn't meant to be

Oh! My precious darling
Our home is lonely today
The chair that you sat in
Reminds me of you each day

Good night my love
I must retire now
Perhaps I'll dream of you
And I'll face tomorrow some how

No. 130 - December 16, 1998 – Age 88

92

Memories IV

Memories keep coming back
Of the things you did for me
Tears of happiness filled my eyes
So I could hardly see

You took me to church my darling
And we heard Pastor Gooding sing
You bought and gave me gifts
You bought me lamps and everything

You bought me lamps
You bought me dishes
You tried to fulfill
All my wishes

You bought me carpets
To cover the floor
Then you asked me
If I needed anything more

You buried rocks in the yard
You put them out of sight
You came and worked on the house
After work each night

So tonight I go
Back in memory
And think of the man
That was so good to me

No. 131 - December 16, 1998 – Age 88

On a cold and snow covered Saturday night, December 21, 1957, Ivar and Helen entered into matrimony. They promised to love each other to the end and that is exactly what they did. The author at the age of 15 stood up for them. No one could ever ask for a more caring step-dad.

It Was December 21ˢᵗ, 1957

It was forty-one years ago
When I heard you say I do
It seemed I was in Heaven
It was too good to be true

You stood so close beside me
Oh! Your blond curly hair
And I was so happy
You were standing there

I wore a blue lace dress
That night so long ago
I never dreamed I could be so happy
God willed it to be so

Many years we spent together
Sometimes laughing sometimes to cry
You were a faithful husband
Up to the day you had to die

I'll never forget you darling
I'll never forget your face
And no other man
Can ever take your place

Good night my precious darling
It's sad we had to part
But forever and forever
You will remain in my heart

No. 132 - December 18, 1998 – Age 88

A Picture Of My Darling

I have a picture of my darling
I sit it where I can see
As I pass by it each day
It always smiles at me

You were so handsome my darling
I sit it on a stand
And each and every day I thank
God for giving me such a wonderful man

As I pass it each
And every day
Tears fill my eyes
And I brush them away

Oh! My precious darling
You were so good to me
But you had to leave our home
God willed it to be

Your picture is only made of paper
But I cherish it each day
And I will always wonder
Why you were called away

Good night my precious darling
I miss you so my dear
And as I look at your picture
I wish you were here

No. 136 - December 22, 1998 – Age 88

He Was Special

It was so special
The love we had then
And I know I will never
Find another like him

He was special
To me all the time
He was a special man
And he was mine

He was so special
In every way
And no other can take the place
Of the man I had one day

He was so kind and honest
And so good too
Oh! That special man
Brought me a love so true

He was my loving husband
He was my friend
I never dreamed that one day
Our love would end

My special man
Was called away
Now I have only his picture
To look at each day

No. 137 - December 23, 1998 – Age 88

Lasting Memories

When the day is ending
They return to me
Once again I recall
Those lasting memories

And as the leaves fall
From off the trees
I go back in memory
To those lasting memories

When the grass is green
And robins start to sing
And the squirrels are so free
Once again I have those lasting memories

And the roses bloom
Early in the spring we see
All of these beautiful things
Remind me of lasting memories

When the whippoorwill
Sings a lovely song
Lasting memories come to me
And stay with me all day long

Oh! My precious darling
For you I long to see
I try to forget, I try to forget
But it will forever be lasting memories

No. 138 - December 30, 1998 – Age 88

98

Six

The Year 1999

This photograph was taken in June 1961. It shows how neat Ivar kept the lawn and the flower boxes around the edge of the terrace. The terrace was built around a very large Oak and an Elm tree. They helped to shade the house most of the day. This was also after they had it re-shingled and an antique silver stain applied. Ivar and Helen were very proud of the appearance of their property.

My Heart Belongs To You

Oh! My precious darling
We had a love so true
May I say once again
My heart belongs to you

Eleven years have passed
Since God called you home
Oh! My precious darling
I'm so lonely and alone

You were so brave my dear
You knew you were going to die
Now in the evening light
Loneliness may make me cry

Yes my precious darling
And every day through
I long to see you again to
Tell you my heart still belongs to you

Those precious, precious times
When you took care of me
They are gone forever more
And again they can never be

Goodnight my precious darling
Wherever you may be
I hope you are happy there
Since you cannot live with me

No. 140 - January 14, 1999 – Age 88

January 21 – Eleventh Anniversary

Lonely Nights Without You

I face each lonely night
Without you
Your chair is empty now
I'm lonely all night through

As I recall the day you left
I feel so all alone
This house is just a house
When it used to be a home

Oh! How can I go on
And face each lonely day
Since my darling you're not here
For you were called away

I sit in the den
And I watch TV
Now my precious darling
You cannot be with me

Oh! My precious darling
The nights are so lonely too
Since I sit in the den alone
When I used to sit there with you

Good night my love
I want to say good night to you
I'll always remember I once had
A love that was so true

No. 148 - March 15, 1999 – Age 88

This photograph was taken in July 1954 on the terrace outside her house. This was a time when Helen was left alone to care for and support her two sons. She cleaned houses to earn money to keep the household running. Having to push a Reo mower and short of time from working, the grass had gotten the better of her as can be seen to the left of the house, how tall it has grown. Three and a half years later her life would turn around as she became Helen O. Larson.

This is a photograph of the original rings they gave each other on that December night. Helen speaks of them in the poem on the facing page. The author found them in a little box in a dresser drawer in her bedroom. On top of the dresser was the picture of Ivar in a gold frame, see page 26.

My House Is Not A Home

Today the sun is shining
The birds are singing too
All nature is so happy
While I am so blue for you

The grass is turning green
It needs some care again
I remember when you used to mow it
Again and again

My house is so empty
And so quiet too
Not a sound can be heard
So once more I miss you

Will things ever change
Will it ever seem like a home
Maybe I'll be lonely forever
For you're not in my home

Often I look at your picture
Often I look at our rings
So often I think of you
Only heart-break it brings

Good night my precious darling
It was meant to be
That you had to leave our home
And you can never be with me

No. 149 - March 16, 1999 – Age 88

This photograph of Helen O. Wolf was taken in her front yard the winter of 1956. She and Ivar had been dating seven months since that fateful day in April. Little did she know, approximately one year later, she would become Helen O. Larson for ever more.

Snow On The Pine Trees

When the snow falls
And covers every pine tree
That's the time I want to
Have you here with me

Children will be playing
And sliding in the snow
And forever and forever
I'll be longing for you

I miss the quiet evenings
And holding hands with you
My heart aches
Each day through

Oh! If only one more day
Just one more time
I could have once more
That love of mine

It's so lonely my darling
I miss you so my dear
And no one knows how I long
To have you here

My life is filled with heart aches
Each and every day
Oh! My precious darling
You're so far away

Good night my precious love
The stars will soon appear
And I'll just have to
Make believe you're here

No. 152 - March 24, 1999 – Age 88

It Was Only A Dream

We were walking down a lane
Holding each other's hand
We saw the beautiful flowers
Growing on the land

Soon it would be dark
And the stars would come out
And the night owls would be
Heard without a doubt

Then the moon would appear
So bright in the sky
And no one else around
Just you and I

Oh! It was so beautiful
Walking there with you
Oh! My precious darling
It was a dream come true

Then it was time to go home
Once more to say goodbye
It was a happy wonderland
With the moon and stars in the sky

But I awoke in the morning
And found it was only a dream
All of natures beauty
That I had seen

No. 153 - March 25, 1999 – Age 88

Old Memories Never Die

All these memories keep coming back
To me each day
Memories of a true love
That passed away

Memories of a time
So very long ago
When I was a prisoner in my home
Because of so much snow

Memories of a time
When my children were young
Memories of both of
My handsome sons

Memories of a time
I had my husband with me
Now those memories are sad
For destiny took him from me

When I think of all those old memories
My heart aches once again
For those old memories
I spent with him

I go back each day and live those memories once more
And all those happy times I spent with him before

Memories of when we went to yard sales and bought some
pretty things
Oh! Those memories of long ago, tears to my heart they bring

Again today I am recalling, old memories gone by
And as we all know, old memories never die

No. 154 - April 8, 1999 – Age 88

When Flowers Bloom

When the flowers bloom
All colors of red and blue
That's the time my darling
That I long to see you

When the roses bloomed
Is when I met you
At last I found
A love so true

Oh! Each time I see the roses
My heart aches once more
For I had so much happiness
In those days before

And when I see the lilies
So pure and so white
I long to live once again
In that moon light

When the violets bloom
With the color blue
Oh! My darling once again
I long to see you

Oh! My darling the flowers
Are going to bloom again one day
And I'll be broken hearted
Because you went away

No. 155 - April 13, 1999 – Age 88

108

Bouquet Of Roses

You sent me a bouquet of roses
They were the color of blue
I loved and cherished them
Because they came from you

I set them on a table
In an antique vase
And each time I smelled the roses
I longed to see your face

Oh! The beautiful roses
I watered them each day
And when they died I cried
For I had to throw them away

Oh! Those beautiful roses
You were so kind to send them
But after all
You are a special man

Oh! The beautiful roses
That you sent me one day
I loved them so much
But they withered away

We were so in love
And happy all the time
And I had you many years
And you were mine all mine

No. 165 - April 19, 1999 – Age 88

This photograph was taken of Ivar and Helen by the author in the summer of 1956. It is apparent the love that they shared as they dated for the next year. The location was in what was known as Keenan's Pasture. Ed Keenan's cows used to roam everywhere on the property. This site is now owned by the author.

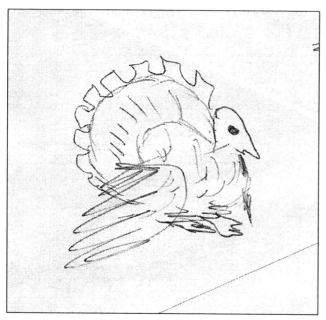

Gramma Larson, as she was called, used to love to draw this turkey for her grand children. She would draw it in less than a minute and then give it to them so they could keep it. Having lived thru the Great Depression in the 1930s, Gramma hardly ever wasted anything. This was drawn on the back of a used envelope.

Then God Sent Me You

I had been so lonely
All my life through
Then one day many years ago
God sent me you

No one seemed to want to be my friend
I didn't know what to do
Then one day in April
I stepped on your bus and met you

Yes, many years I was lonely
Then I met my best friend
And we lived and loved each other
Right to the end

I'll never forget that day in April
So many years ago
When destiny stepped in
And allowed it to be so

We watched TV together
And you held my hand
Yes, it was a lucky day
When I met my special man

I'll always remember
The day you came into my life
I'll always remember
The night I became your wife

No. 169 - May 8, 1999 – Age 88

Good Night Darling

When the moon comes up
Over the deep blue sea
That's when I long
To have you here with me

When the sea gulls cry
That's when I cry too
For my dearest darling
I long to see you

When the tide comes in
And washes against the shore
I want to be with
You once more

I miss you so my darling
My home is empty now
Each day brings me sadness
But I get through it some how

I wonder why you
Were taken away from me
And when I cry my darling
Through the tears I cannot see

Good night my love
Good night my dear
I miss you so
And I long to have you near

No. 170 - May 10, 1999 – Age 88

I Walk Alone III

When the day starts
I walk alone
For one January day
God called you home

I see the birds
And the sunshine
But I lost that
Great love of mine

The sky is gray
It is never blue
Since that January day
That I lost you

My darling I try but
Life isn't the same now
But I manage to
Get through some how

So many places
We went together dear
Is it any wonder why
I want you near

Another day is starting
It's lonesome in my home
Another day of sorrow
Since God called you home

No. 173 - May 12, 1999 – Age 88

Helen is seen here posing for this photograph taken in June 1951. She was on the swing in the front yard. Later that year she would be left alone to fend for herself and her two boys ages nine and fifteen.

I Want To Walk Again With You

Let me once more walk the trail with you
Let me once more walk down that lane where I walked
with my love so true

I often day dream I am walking in the park with you
Maybe one of these days my dream will come true

I really miss the walks I used to take with you
But maybe I will have a dream that will come true

Yes, I want to walk again in the moon light with you
And have you near me too, all day, every day through

Yes, I'll forever want to walk along life's road with you
Some day my darling it may come true

Once more, one more day, one more hour, one more time
Always the same walk with that love of mine

No. 181 - May 16 & 17, 1999 – Age 88

When The Roses Bloom

When the roses bloom again
And the winter is through
I know you my darling
Yes, you'll be coming too

You will bring a bouquet
And knock on my door
You'll be here and I will
Be happy once more

I am waiting for
The roses to bloom again
For I know when they do
You'll return again

Yes, I will keep on waiting
For the roses to bloom
It has been raining
So I know it will be soon

Yes, soon the roses
Will bloom once more
That's the time
You'll be knocking on my door

When the roses bloom
My darling I'll think of you
Forever and ever you're on my mind
You were my love so true

No. 183 - May 22 & 23, 1999 – Age 88

The Heart Ache No One Can Erase

When evening comes and all is still
And stars appear in the sky
I go over the events of my life
And wonder why

Why were there so many things
That caused my heart to ache
Why all these tragedies
Was it all because of fate

The sun is shining
The flowers are blooming too
Its spring time every where
So today I think of you

I think of all the good times
When you were here with me
But one day my darling
Our love wasn't meant to be

God took you away
You were only 72
Oh! My precious darling
It's so lonely without you

I try to go on with a smile on my face
But my heart-ache, no one can erase

The days are long, I miss you so my dear
And no one knows how I wish you were here

I'll get through the day and do what I have to do
But only God and the Angels know how very much I miss you

No. 187 - May 28, 1999 – Age 88

Foot Prints On My Heart

He came into my life
But one day we had to part
And the day that he left
He left foot prints on my heart

I remember the sound of
His footsteps coming up to the door
I was happy when I heard them
But I don't hear them anymore

I would be so happy
If I could hear them one day
But that can never happen
For God called you away

We had such good times
Going here and there
I am so sad when
I see his empty chair

He was the kind of friend
That you never forget
And the foot prints that he left
Are on my heart yet

We used to watch TV holding hands each night
Oh! That precious friend of mine did everything just right

My dearest friend and I, one day we had to part
But the day he went away, he left foot prints on my heart

We used to go to yard sales to buy a treasure or two
And if I could only tell him, the foot prints on my heart
were left there by you

No. 208 - June 18, 1999 – Age 88

Helen and Ivar on their wedding day, December 21, 1957.

My Best Friend

Oh! Those years of sorrow came to an end
The blessed day that I met my best friend

I told him about my sorrow, he said I've had sorrow too
And if you will marry me I'll be good to you

Thirty-one years we were married, we were together right to the end
And the day I lost him I lost my best friend

No one knows how I miss him and how I wish he was here
But God called away, the one that was so dear

I'll miss him forever; maybe I'll see him some day
I have to go on living, longing for my friend that was taken away

Oh! My precious darling you were the only one
That started being good to me the day our marriage had begun

No. 210 - June 25, 1999 – Age 88

118

That Night In December

Oh! That night in December
Forty-one years ago
Was a happy occasion
God had willed it so

The Christmas trees were up
The lights did shine
And on that night in December
He became mine

When I think of the happiness
Of that night of so long ago
I miss that man that married me
More than anyone will know

I go back in memory
Of the years I spent with him
Oh! If only I could spend
One more day with him

My darling was with me
The ground was covered with snow so white
But we were so happy
On that cold December night

Oh! That night in December
Is in my memory to stay
And the months and years
Can never take it away

No. 223 - July 28, 1999 – Age 88

You're Just Away

I miss you my darling
Each and every day
But I know I'll see you
Again some day

My darling you are
Not gone forever dear
Though I can't see you
I feel you are very near

I remember the last days
I spent with you
Just before your life
Was through

Oh! My precious Ivar
I miss you and your kind ways
Since you had to go away
These are lonely days

My darling Ivar
It's so lonely now
But with my faith in God
I get through some how

Again today I'm thinking
Of when you were here
I love and miss you darling
And I wish you were near

No. 232 - August 5, 1999 – Age 88

120

I Found Love One Day

One day in April
I stepped on a bus to take a ride
And the driver looked at me
And his love he could not hide

He said good morning
How are you today
And on that April morning
I fell in love right away

He was a handsome man
With blond curly hair
And I'll always cherish the day
I saw him sitting there

After a few days he asked
If he could come and see me
And then he came one night
And I was happy as could be

He asked me if I would
Marry him one day
And my answer was yes
I'll marry you right away

And we were married on a cold December night
The Christmas trees were lit up with lights that shone so bright

I'll forever miss him; he'll forever be with me
Every day in my heart, though his face I cannot see

I'll forever love him and long to see his face
There is no other that can take his place

No. 234 - August 11, 1999 – Age 88

Footprints In The Snow

If you could walk up the path
And leave foot prints in the snow
It would make me so happy
If you could do so

If you could walk to the garage
And leave your footprints there one day
I would again be happy and
I'd wish they would never melt away

If we could go together
And cut the Christmas tree
Your footprints would be in the snow
As you walked along beside me

When I saw the snow falling
Once more I'd be happy
For I would know by your footprints
You were coming to see me

You will never return
You can never come back I know
But I will always long to see
Your footprints in the snow

So my precious darling
I'm waiting for it to snow again
Although I know you can never
Make footprints in the snow again

No. 238 - August 24, 1999 – Age 88

Footprints In The Sand

If I could only walk by the sea
Holding your hand
If I could only see
Your footprints in the sand

I know it can never happen
And you can't walk there with me
But I still long to walk
With you by the sea

If only once
Just one more time
I could walk with you for
You were that great love of mine

We could watch the waves
Coming against the shore
Oh! To walk there with you
Just once more

But it can never happen, destiny stepped in
And took you away from me
So my darling we can never
Walk again by the sea

I'll forever long
To have this wish come true
To once, just once more
Walk by the sea with you

No. 240 - August 26, 1999 – Age 88

This is one view Helen had when she would lay on her bed and look out the window. She would see the garage where her precious Ivar would make things. He would make ornaments for the lawn or shelves for the lamps in the house. He was always tinkering in the garage to make something for her.

When Skies Are Blue

When the sun is shining
And the skies are blue
My dearest darling
I long to see you

When I look around and see
The things you used to do
My heart aches once again
My darling to see you

I see the garage where
You made things each day
You did so many things
Before you passed away

I miss the times
You took me out each day
I miss your loving smile
Since you passed away

You used to vacuum
Each floor
And now since you are gone
You can't vacuum any more

I miss so many things
That you used to do
But darling most of all
I miss you

No. 248 - August 29, 1999 – Age 88

It Hurt To Say Good-bye

My darling was so sick so
To the hospital he went one day
When he left home he said
It will be a short stay

Day after day went by
The weeks went too
I was sick and depressed
And I didn't know what to do

I couldn't visit him often
I couldn't walk to good then
But I managed to visit him once
And then once more again

After eight weeks had passed
And they could do no more for him
I told the doctors I wanted
To bring him home again

So I brought him home
And watched day after day
As his precious life
Was slipping away

Finally the end came
I was heart-broken but couldn't cry
And on that January day
It hurt to say good-bye

No. 255 - September 7, 1999 – Age 88

My Guardian

I call him my guardian
He was so good to me
He watched over me each day
He was good as could be

He bought me gifts
Of most any kind
And I loved that
Very good man of mine

I miss him, I miss him
More than anyone can know
I feel so sad because
He had to go

All the years I had him
He was gentle and kind
And a good man like him
Would be hard to find

As long as I live
He will remain in my heart
And I remember the sad day
That we had to part

I look at his picture
Every now and then
And my heart aches
For I can't see him again

No. 257 - September 9, 1999 – Age 88

Someday We'll Meet Again

Someday my precious darling
We will meet once more
When our life is over
And we'll love as before

We'll once again hold hands
And together we'll watch TV
It will be so wonderful
To have you again with me

We'll go for long rides
In the country dear
Oh! You can never know
How much I want you near

I remember that smile
I remember so many things about you
I used to love to watch
The things you used to do

We could go to yard sales
And buy some nice things
Oh! When I think of all the good times
Happiness to me it brings

I can go on wishing
And someday it may come true
And hoping that someday
It will come true

No. 261 - September 20, 1999 – Age 88

128

He Knows Everything

He knows when I am lonely
He knows when I am blue
He knows the heart-ache
Since I lost you

He knows I really try
To get through the day
He knows if I cry
I'll brush the tears away

I know He hears
Me when I pray
And He always listens
To me each day

He knows how
Much I miss you
My special love
So great and true

I know that sometime
I'll be free from pain
I know that one day
I'll see you again

So I'll try to go on
And pray each day
For I know that one day
He'll brush my tears away

No. 264 - September 24, 1999 – Age 88

129

Help Me Through This Lonely Night

I sit alone in my home
In the evening light
Please help me to
Get through this lonely night

Let me make believe you're with me
As the moon is shining bright
Help me bare the pain and heart-ache
As the stars twinkle in the night

Oh! My precious darling when you were with me
Everything was all right
Help me, please help me
Make it through this night

Once again I ask you
Think of me in the candle light
Oh! My precious darling
Think of me this night

Forever and forever I'll miss you
Especially when its moon light
Once more my darling I ask you
To come and see me tonight

Often I think of you
You did everything right
And with the memories of you
I will make it through this night

No. 271 - November 1999 – Age 89

Seven

The End Is Near

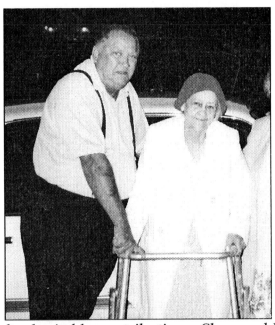

Helen often made charitable contributions. She would enclose one of her religious poems. Her goal was to have one of her poems in every state. (The author completed her goal.) One particular time, the girl that opened her envelope to remove the money order, threw the poem in the waste basket. Another worker saw it in the basket and thought her dad, being a minister, would enjoy reading it and took it home. Her dad was Jeff Barbour and Paul Barbour (pictured above) was Jeff's dad, both of Winchester, Virginia. Paul tracked Helen down through information and called her. He wanted her permission to read the poem to his son's congregation. They became very good friends and for his 70th birthday he wanted his son to bring him to Rhode Island to meet Helen. On September 15, 2001 Jeff drove him here to meet her. This photograph was taken as they were entering the restaurant they took Helen to that night. On October 24th Helen turned 91. Paul passed away soon after.

I Long To See You

The sun is going down
I'm alone tonight
I keep thinking of the nights
We spent in the moon light

My home is empty now
That you have gone
It used to be so nice eating
Breakfast with you each morn

I look at the bed
Where you used to sleep
And if I could cry
Many tears I would weep

Oh! My precious darling
No one will ever know
How I long to see you
Since you had to go

The house is lonely now
I miss your footsteps coming to the door
Oh! My precious darling
I long to see you once more

Life can be so lonely
If you don't have someone to love
It's good to know that I can talk
To Jesus up above

No. 281 - February 2000 – Age 89

To Have Him Home Again

The sun is shining
And I'm all alone
Thinking of the man
Who shared my home

It was many years ago
That God called him away
And I have been so lonely
Since that sad day

The grass will
Soon be green
To have him back again
Is my only dream

I know I am wishing
For something that cannot be
But I'll keep wishing
To have him here with me

To know he is here
In my home once more
To hear his loving foot steps
As he comes up to the door

It was so sad for me on that January day
Twelve years ago when God called him away

I often think of the years that he was in my home
Now there's an empty feeling since I am all alone

So I go on thinking how nice it would be
To have him here living with me

No. 284 - March 26, 2000 – Age 89

This is the window Helen would look out as she lay on her bed taking her afternoon rest. I'm sure she longed to see Ivar drive up that drive way, open the door, and say he was home. It had been over twelve long years since he had done so when she wrote the poem on the facing page.

I Had To Say Goodbye

I'm thinking of you my darling
Each hour of the day
And I often wonder why
You were taken away

The days are lonely now
The nights are lonely too
For each and every day
And every hour I think of you

The sky is blue
The birds do sing
But all of these wonders
To me don't mean a thing

I look out the window
And see the path each day
Oh! How my heart cries
Since you went away

We sat on the couch
Holding each other's hand
You were my special love
You were my special man

As long as I live
My heart will cry
For to my great love
I had to say goodbye

No. 288 - April 2000 - Age 89

Please Ask The Angels To Move Over

Oh! My precious darling
I brought you home to die
My heart was breaking
But I could not cry

Oh! How I watched you
As you laid there
And I knelt beside your bed
And said a prayer

You were so very sick
You knew you had to go
I knew I was going to lose you
For God had willed it to be so

Oh! My precious darling
The days are lonely now
But with the help of Jesus
I'll get through some how

I look out the window and see
The little path that leads to the door
Then my heart aches once again
For you don't walk on it any more

I know there is a Heaven
Where there is no sin
Jesus, please ask the Angels to more over
And make room for him

No. 290 - May 26, 2000 – Age 89

I'll Never Forget You

The sun is shining today
And I am all alone
I keep thinking of the time
That you were in our home

I'm thinking of the days
We were happy you and I
When I never needed
To break down and cry

You were so good to me
From heart-break I was free
But that was a long time ago
It was destroyed by destiny

Oh! My precious darling
The sky is no longer blue
Since that heart-breaking day
That I lost you

I'm looking out the window
And maybe I will see
A little squirrel running
So happy and free

Memories keep coming back of days of long ago
When I had your love and you had mine you know

People tell me to forget, they don't know what they say
For I will never forget you till my dying day

So long my darling, until another time
And for thirty-one years, you were mine, all mine

No. 295 - June 24, 2000 – Age 89

This photograph was taken in December 1990. It shows Helen holding her first great-grandchild, Justin Wolf. With her are her son Raymond and her grandson Joel J. Wolf, Justin's father. Beside her are a number of doilies she crocheted along with pot holders and afghans. They were most likely Christmas gifts for friends and family. Even at eighty she enjoyed making things and giving them to friends and relatives as gifts, all year long. On the bookcase behind the author can be seen a lone lamp from her extensive lamp collection.

I Dreamed Of You Last Night

Oh! My precious darling
I dreamed of you last night
Oh! It was so wonderful
Your arms around me tight

You began to cry, you were
So happy to see me
I thought I would cry too my love
I was so happy you came to see me

God allowed us to meet
For such a short time
Oh! My precious darling
Once you were mine, all mine

I remember I told you
I loved you as before
And that I miss your footsteps
Coming up to the door

I didn't want the dream
To come to an end
For my darling
You were my best friend

Soon I awoke and
You were gone my dear
But I have precious memories
Of when you were here

No. 298 - December 2000 – Age 90

Helen was admitted to Rhode Island Hospital on January 21, 2002 with Pneumonia. After a short stay she was transported to Cra-Mar Nursing Home on January 29th to regain her strength. On February 2nd the author woke up from a sound sleep, grabbed a pen and pad and wrote the following poem in about five minutes. He believes she mentally dictated it to him considering this was the first poem he had ever written. Everyone felt, she being 91, that this was the best place for Helen to live her remaining years. However, she disagreed and finally convinced him and he took her home February 16th. Most of Helen's poems in 2002 were religious; she did not write one poem about Ivar.

My Days At Cra-Mar

The lady with the hair brush
Keeps my hair so neat
She comes around each morning
Just before I eat

Then I lay here each day
Thinking of yesteryear
And then all of a sudden
To my eyes come a tear

I have lived a long time
100 my son says I will be
But today I'm only 91
And I just want to be free

Raymond will be in soon
He comes every day
And soon I know he will bring
My beautiful Ashlee Rae

He says if I get stronger
I can go home
Then I will call all my friends
And talk forever on the phone

I'm in Cra-Mar Nursing Home
And the people are so nice
The only problem is
The awfully high price

Medicaid is paying
Because I'm smart you see
I gave my house to Raymond
So that I could live free

I'm getting really tired
And think I'll lay down to sleep
Only nine more years Lord
Then I'll no longer weep

Then one day, I'll come home to you
Through those pearly gates, to meet Ivar and Elvis too

But until then I will praise your name
That whatever happens to this World, you are not to blame

February 2, 2002 – by Ray Wolf

January of 2003 Helen was admitted to Rhode Island Hospital again with pneumonia. Once more on January 23rd she re-entered Cra-Mar Nursing Home. While she was there she wrote the following five poems expressing her desire to be at her home pictured above. The author really believed, this time at 92, Cra-Mar was her final residence. However, she kept saying she did not belong there and that she got her strength back before at home and she could do it again. Finally after convincing him, February 15th he took her home. When Helen was at home she wrote a number of poems including the two on pages 148 and 149 about being home. Because these two poems and the five she wrote while at Cra-Mar are not of Ivar they are not numbered. On page 150 is the only one she wrote about her Ivar in 2003. This photograph was taken April 2005. (Courtesy of Kimberly Roderick.)

2004 was a good year; she made it past January with no illness. The only poem she wrote about her Ivar was on January 21st the 16th anniversary of his passing. It was her 300th poem written about him. At 93, approaching 94, she was visibly slowing down, but still living by herself in the home she loved and helped build sixty-two years ago.

Return To My Home

I'm home-sick dear friend
And I have to hold back the tears
I'm home-sick, yes, I am
For my home of 60 years

Each day my heart aches
For that home of mine
I brush the tears away
Time after time

Maybe one day Jesus will heal
My body once again
And each day, I will pray
And give thanks to Him

So until that happens
I'll try to face each day
And try to make believe
It will be a short stay

Jesus, help me to go on
Each day I'm away
And pray I may return
To my home one day

January 26, 2003 - Age 92

January 21 – Fifteenth Anniversary

Written at Cra-Mar Nursing Home

My Home On Richard Street

My home on Richard Street
I wish I were there
Jesus, you understand
So I go to you in prayer

The days are long and lonely
As I sit each day here
I'm so glad I have you
A friend so dear

Lay your hands on my body
And with your healing power
Restore my health dear Jesus
Each and every hour

They do not know I have a friend
So gentle, kind and true
And any hour of the day
I can pray and talk to you

Stay close beside me
So each day I can make it through
For I know my friends name
Is Jesus, so kind and true

January 27, 2003 - Age 92

Written at Cra-Mar Nursing Home

Out The Door

I am away from home
Through no fault of my own
They brought me here one day
I hope it won't be a long stay

They do not know the heart-ache
I suffer each day
For the six room home
I left one January day

The nurses are nice
The food is good too
But I'd rather be home
You would too

I sit each lonely hour
In this room at Cra-Mar
I can't change anything
So they'll stay as they are

I am a prisoner
Locked here today
Away from my home
Not far away

I will pray I keep
A sound mind
And one day I will walk out the door
And leave this room behind

January 28, 2003 - Age 92

Written at Cra-Mar Nursing Home

Open The Door

Let me open the door of my home
And walk in one day
Let me walk in the bedroom
And see the bed where I used to lay

Let me see each
Room in my home
Where I was happy
And never left alone

Every room in my home
Is so precious to me
Let it be dear God
Let it be, let it be

Dear God let this heart-ache
Leave me one day
Let me leave my prison
Let it be a short stay

My son Ray came to see me
Once again today
His loving smiles helps
To make the time pass away

Let me walk out in the yard
And see the birds as they fly
Oh dear God in heaven
Let me be in my home when I die

January 29, 2003 - Age 92

Written at Cra-Mar Nursing Home

The Male Nurse

I do not know the man
I do not know his name
When he walks in the room
I have a feeling I can't explain

He seems so gentle and kind
He has a healing effect on me
I don't know how to tell you
But God seems to let it be

And for a few days
He went away
But yesterday he returned
I hope this time to stay

Dear God I thank you
For sending him into my room again
Each day I'll pray and thank you
For sending him

So God I ask you
Watch over him each day
And I'll include him in my prayers
Each time I pray

Dear God I believe
You gave a healing touch to him one day
And I pray he'll be here
All during my stay

January 29, 2003 - Age 92

Written at Cra-Mar Nursing Home

God Unlocked The Door of My Prison

God released me from my prison
He unlocked the door one day
I got in my sons car
And we drove away

I'm in my home now
It's where I prayed to be
I'm living alone but happy
That one day I became free

I looked out the window
As I sat in my chair each day
Longing to be home on Richard Street
That wasn't far away

I used to pray for mercy
To come to me
And one day my prayer was answered
I left that place where I wasn't free

You couldn't talk to the people
They wouldn't understand what you had to say
And now when it comes night again
In my own bed I can lay

I am so thankful to be home
It's where I belong
And to stay in a nursing home
Was absolutely wrong

June 5th and 6th 2003 - Age 92

Written at home

It's Good To Be Home

It's good to be home each day
Where my heart has always been
And I pray I will never have to go
To a nursing home again

I can eat when I want
Each and every day
And when the nighttime comes
In my own bed I can lay

I feel sorry for all those people
That are there and can't go home
They must be very home sick
They must feel all alone

I can look out the window
Each and every day
I can see the little squirrels
As they run and play

I can look out the window
In the home that I love
And when nighttime comes
I can gaze at the stars above

I thank the Lord Jesus
For answering my prayer
I'm home where I belong
And I'm no longer there

November 2003 – Age 93

Written at home

You're Still In My Heart

You're still in my heart my darling
And forever and ever you'll be
It is so sad my love
That you had to leave me

I remember the day so well
When we had to say good-bye
You left me with a broken heart
The day you had to die

I brought you home my dear
It's where you wanted to be
You were so happy dear
To be back home with me

The days and months have passed
And the years have passed too
But they can never take away
My memories of you

The table is no longer in the kitchen
So I don't have to see your empty chair
Each day and every day
Because you always sat there

I will go on living
With a broken heart
Because 15 years ago
God decided we should part

No. 299 - December 30, 2003 - Age 93

150

You Have Never Left My Heart

You departed from the Earth
But we have never been apart
For my dearest darling
You have never left my heart

I met you on a bus
It was an April day
I didn't know that some time
You would come to me to stay

We talked a lot that day
You asked if you could come see me
Yes my dearest darling
It was destiny

I said you could come
And cut some trees down
I didn't know it then
But my true love I had found

Then one day you asked me
Would I marry you
My answer was yes
For I found my love so true

And so we were married on a December night
The Christmas tree was up with candles sparkling light

No one knows the longing that is forever in my heart
Ever since you were taken away and we had to part

No. 300 - January 21, 2004 - Age 93

January 21 – Sixteenth Anniversary

January 2005 came and went with no incident and looked like another good year for Helen. But fate had other plans. On March 3rd she was taken to Rhode Island Hospital again for a very short stay. Then a trip to the Haven Health Center in Coventry followed, pictured above, on March 6th. Her son reasoned that in 2002 he took her home from Cra-Mar Nursing Home and she did well for a year. Then in 2003 when he again took her home she was great for two more years. Now on April 7, 2005 he took her home again but neither one of them was certain that this time she could get her strength back. On April 13th she re-entered Rhode Island Hospital again and on April 14th she re-entered Haven Health Center for the final time. While she was home, from April 7th to April 13th, she was cared for by a lady named Alice. On April 14th her son asked her to compose a poem about Alice. She wrote a few lines for him that day and on the 15th when he was visiting her she finished the verses of the poem. The completed poem is on the facing page.

Alice

Her name is Alice
She came to see me one day
I am so sorry
She couldn't stay

Things didn't work out
The way we thought they would
But you and I know
That they certainly should

She was so nice
I loved it when she came
Now Alice is gone
Isn't it a shame

Alice is so thoughtful
And also so kind
And another like her
Would be hard to find

Just a few days
She stayed with me
But she really had to go
For it was meant to be

So long Alice
I'm so glad we met
Though the years roll by
You're one grand person I won't forget

April 14th and 15th 2005 - Age 94

Written at Haven Health Center

This photograph was taken April 16, 2005 at the Haven Health Center. Helen's granddaughter Ashlee Rae Wolf and Tyler Roderick are with Helen and the author. Tyler was interviewing Helen for a book report he was doing for one of his classes in school. This photograph was taken exactly one month before she would spiritually dictate her final poem to the author on May 16th.

He was with Helen when she passed away on May 18th as Elvis was singing Amazing Grace on the CD player on the night stand beside her bed. The picture of Elvis on the facing page almost seems like he is singing directly to her.

Helen donated her body to Brown Medical Center in Providence, Rhode Island. She did not want a funeral or a wake. Her attitude was, "If they didn't come to see me when I was alive, then I don't want to see them when I'm dead." She ordered not to post a notice of her death in the paper for fear someone would break into her unoccupied home and steal her collection of Blue Willow dinnerware. All of her wishes were carried out. A very small memorial service was held at the author's home on June 5, 2005 as shown on page 158. (Courtesy of Kimberly Roderick.)

The author took this photograph of Elvis performing at the Providence Civic Center in Rhode Island on June 22, 1974. Although Gramma never was able to see him perform on stage, she loved him singing gospel music and watched videos of his movies and concerts. She admired how much he loved his mother. Elvis always ended his concerts with the song *Can't Help Falling In Love* from his 1961 movie Blue Hawaii.

On Saturday morning May 16th the author was sitting beside her bed. He picked up a pen and pad and wrote the second poem of his life. For the next hour and a half as she lay sleeping, unconscious, he would write a few lines, put the pen down, then pick it up and write a few more. He titled it *Couldn't Help Falling In Love.* The next page begins this books final poem. Helen never regained consciousness and passed away two days later. The author will always believe she spiritually dictated this poem to him as he believes she did the first poem he ever wrote, seen on pages 140-141. (Used with permission of Elvis Presley Enterprises, Inc.)

Couldn't Help Falling In Love

Elvis I love you
And soon we will meet
Together hand in hand
We will walk God's golden street

Meet me at Heaven's gate
And open it for me
Please Elvis be singing Amazing Grace
For it is my favorite Hymn you see

I have lived a long time
And loved you over half my years
When you sing How Great Thou Art
To my eyes it brings tears

Introduce me to Jesus
Such a good friend he's been to me
Always there when I needed him
And now will set me free

Your fans still miss you
But not as much as I
And soon we will be
Together in the sky

I am now listening to your CD
Whatever that is
With my son Raymond
His visits with me I will miss

My time on God's Earth
Is getting short
I am so happy that
Your records and tapes I bought

They comforted me so
When my spirits were down
I would sit and listen
As they went round and round

My grandson Joel
Was born January 8th
The date you were born in Tupelo
He and Tonya will soon have their fourth

My son Raymond and Ramona
Were married on the 16th of August
Such a sad day in history
The date you were called to leave us

I cannot drink
And I cannot eat
I can only lay here
Can't even feel my feet

Over the years almost seventeen hundred
Poems I have been writing
Some of you, some of Jesus
Others of my life, family and any happening

As I go to sleep
And this poem closed my book to you
I will be dreaming of meeting
My love Ivar, my son Paul, Jesus and Elvis you too

Good Night Elvis

May 16, 2005
As spiritually told to the author by

Helen O. Larson
Age 94 years, 6 months, 25 days
October 24, 1910 – May 18, 2005

Gramma Larson has left the building

From left to right: the author, Helen's brother Harry Groves, his wife Theresa, the author's wife Ramona, Helen's granddaughter Laura Lynn, Ramona's mother Mona Cardente with her husband Domenic, Ashlee, and Reverend Bill Flug presiding. This was in front of the flower garden Ramona and the author made and dedicated in her memory. They included a pine tree that can be seen center right of this picture. It was transplanted from Gramma's property.

It appears to the author the glow the camera picked up in this photograph was actually Helen's spirit watching over everyone as Reverend Flug was reading her last poem that she spiritually dictated to the author.

Memorial Service - June 5, 2005

Eulogy by Laura Lynn Wolf-Olsen, daughter of Paul Wolf.

Where to begin: Gramma was a really remarkable woman. She had her little idiosyncrasies, like we all do, but she also had some amazing qualities and this is why we honor her memory today.

I have memories of Gramma from way back when I was a little kid. I always cherished our visits from New York and being able to spend time with her. We wrote to each other frequently, even through my college years. She would tape quarters to her letters so I would have money for laundry. This was her way of helping me and a gesture that was thoughtful beyond measure.

Gramma was full of stories from her youth and had an absolutely remarkable memory. She remembered things like it was yesterday. She would tell of tales that would make you laugh, cry, or just be amused. Her quick wit and sparkling eyes had a way of capturing your attention and she could keep you occupied with her stories for hours on end.

Gramma also loved to collect things, her spectacular collections of oil lamps and blue willow dishware would make your jaw drop. She loved flea markets and yard sales, bargaining with the person to get a special item for an incredible price, enabling her to grow her collections. I would love taking her to yard sales, she knew the roads of Rhode Island like the back of her hands and she would direct me to every sale on her list, taking out her walker so she could go out to look at the items or if she was too tired, I was directed to bring the item to the car for her to look at. It was always an adventure.

Gramma also taught herself how to crochet, and throughout the years gifted people she loved with a beautiful afghan and matching doilies. Gramma had a giving spirit, if you wanted or needed something that she had, she would give it to you. She also made doilies to give to people that she encountered, as a thank you or just to make them smile. It brought joy to her to be able to share with others. Especially when she shared her poems and love of Jesus with the world around her, sending poems to people all over the country, showing them the love and sacrifice that Jesus made for them and perhaps changing their eternal destiny.

I will miss Gramma, all the little things that we did together but I will keep in my memory how much love she shared with me, how she loved her sons, her grand-kids. How intelligent, gifted, and generous she was and I will see her again in Heaven.

About the Author

Raymond A. Wolf

Raymond A. Wolf is a lifelong resident of Hope, a small village in the Town of Scituate, Rhode Island. He graduated from Scituate High School in 1961 and worked for AAA for 28 years. He retired, after 13 years as a manager of TJ Maxx, to pursue writing books full time. He belongs to six local historical societies and has become passionate about recording local history in the *Images of America* series by Arcadia Publishing. Much of this history is being lost for all time as the older folks are passing on. An equal passion he has is to include some of his mother's poetry in his books. His mom, Helen O. Larson, wrote 1,700 poems in her lifetime. His customers kept asking him when he was going to publish a book of her poems. However, he was unable to find a publisher to pick up on the idea; therefore he had to think out of the box. This is the second book in the *Gramma Larson Remembers* series by Wolf Publishing. The first being, *The Lost Village of Rockland*, released in March 2014.

He lives with his wife Ramona, daughter Ashlee Rae, and Zoey the cat.

Index of Poems

To order any of Ray's books visit:
www.raywolfbooks.com

 The Lost Villages of Scituate: In 1915, the general assembly appointed the Providence Water Supply Board to condemn 14,800 acres of land in rural Scituate. The hardworking people of the five villages were devastated. By December 1916, notices were delivered to the villagers stating that the homes and land they had owned for generations were

 The Scituate Reservoir: In 1772, portions of Providence received water through a system of hollowed out logs. By 1869 the public voted in favor of introducing water into the city from the Pawtuxet River in Cranston. By 1900, it was clear more, and purer water was needed. A public law was approved on April 21, 1915, creating the Providence

 West Warwick: By 1912, the citizens of the western portion of Warwick had been talking about secession. They possessed all the mills on the Pawtuxet River and were largely democratic, while the eastern section was primarily republican. Finally in 1913, the town of West Warwick was incorporated and became the youngest town in the

 Foster: Originally incorporated as part of Scituate in 1731, became a separate community in 1781. The town was named in honor of Theodore Foster, a coauthor of the bill of incorporation. By 1820, the population topped out at 2,900 and then sharply declined. The population would not surpass the 1820 figures until 1975, when it

 Pawtuxet Valley Villages: Between 1806 and 1821, a dozen mills were built on the Pawtuxet River, shaping the economy of surrounding villages. The mills provided a livelihood for the villagers who settled in the valley and drew immigrants looking for a better life from Canada, Italy, Portugal, Sweden, and other faraway countries. For

 *Coventry:* On August 21, 1741, the area west of what is now the town of West Warwick was incorporated into the Township of Coventry. The railroad would traverse Coventry in the mid-1800s, providing the gristmills, sawmills, and farmers with a quicker way to send their goods to market and to receive supplies in return. Along with the

 *The Lost Village of Rockland:* Is a book of 150 photographs & documents with captions, featuring poems and tales by Helen O. Larson. She was born October 24, 1910 and lived in the village of Rockland with her family until the City of Providence Water Supply condemned the land in 1916, by eminent domain, to build the

164